Tormented by PTSD?
Freedom from the War Within

Michael E. Petersen, MSW

PublishAmerica
Baltimore

All Biblical quotes are taken from the King James Version.

First printing

ISBN: 1-4241-0283-9
PUBLISHED BY PUBLISHAMERICA, LLLP
www.publishamerica.com
Baltimore

Printed in the United States of America

I dedicate this book to a special friend, Doug Deacon. His continued friendship over the years has meant a great deal to me. He is no longer with us and wasn't able to read this book, although we talked often about our Vietnam experiences. He left this earth on May 20, 2004 due to a negative reaction to a medication change. "...absent from the body, and to be present with the Lord" (II Corinthians 5:8). He is with his Lord.

Acknowledgements

I first want to thank the Lord Jesus Christ, who has totally changed my life. He saved me from the depths of Hell and delivered me from all negative military memories. He has always been there for me and continually makes intercessions for me. I thank you Jesus for Your forgiveness, love, goodness, and mercy. I love you and await your return.

I want to thank my lovely wife Mary, who has stood by me throughout all these years. Thank you, honey, for always being there as my wife, lover, and mother of my children. Your continual prayer support and encouragement is a great blessing to me. I thank God for the gift He gave me on August 21, 1971, when you became my wife. Thank you again for being my lovely wife. I love you very much.

I want to thank my children (Traci, Erin, Michael, and Maggie) for their continual encouragement over the years and for their love with no resentment to the disability. I thank all of you for your love and strength during the challenging times. I love you so much.

A special thanks to Don Krow, who read a very rough draft and encouraged me to finish the book. Thanks to Greg and Kim Troup; Greg for doing the pictures and Kim for all the computer instructions. I especially want to thank my pastor, Lawson Perdue, Rosalie Joy, and all those who have been praying for me during this time.

I want to give a special thanks to my son-in-law (SSG Thomas M. Barrentine) who has served in Iraq in the war against terrorism and is currently serving his second tour there. Thank you, Tom, and all the men and women who have served in the Armed Forces, whether during peacetime or war. I know that "freedom isn't free." I thank you for your service and sacrifices. Mary and I love you and are praying for you.

Finally, I want to thank PublishAmerica for the opportunity to publish my book.

Foreword

Post Traumatic Stress Disorder (PTSD), also known as "shell shock," is a very real condition. A high percentage of soldiers suffer from PTSD. The Department of Veterans Affairs states that more than half of all male Vietnam veterans and almost half of all female Vietnam veterans—about 1,700,000 Vietnam veterans in all—have experienced "clinically serious stress reaction symptoms." Additionally, 15.2% of all male Vietnam theater veterans (479,000 out of 3,140,000 men who served in Vietnam) and 8.1% of all female Vietnam theater veterans (610 out of 7,200 women who served in Vietnam) are currently diagnosed with PTSD ("Currently" means 1986–88 when the survey was conducted). Forty percent of Vietnam theater veteran men have been divorced at least once (10% had two or more divorces), 14.1% report high levels of marital problems, and 23.1% have high levels of parenting problems. Almost half of all male Vietnam theater veterans currently suffering from PTSD had been arrested or in jail at least once—34.2% more than once—and 11.5% had been convicted of a felony. The estimated lifetime prevalence of alcohol abuse or dependence among male theater veterans is 39.2%, and the estimate for current alcohol abuse or dependence is 11.2%. The estimated lifetime prevalence of drug abuse or dependence among male theater veterans is 5.7%, and the estimate for current drug abuse or dependence is 1.8%.[1] I think you'll agree these statistics are staggering.

http://www.ncptsd.va.gov/facts/general/fs_epidemiological.html

This book is an excellent resource for the person suffering with PTSD and for the pastor or counselor assisting that same person. As a pastor or counselor, we need resources and tools that help us help the people who look to us for advice. Of all the books on the shelves of your library, the one you're holding in your hands will prove to be your most valuable tool when dealing with veterans who suffer with PTSD. Not only that, PTSD is a condition experienced by witnesses of major accidents, natural disasters, and victims of violent crimes.

Tormented by PTSD? is a resource that will improve the lives of countless veterans and military service members for years to come. I've dealt with hundreds of veterans and military service members who would have benefited from the principles and philosophies in this book.

Mike has a knack for presenting the complexities of PTSD in a concise and simple way. Additionally, he provides a typical military style checklist format for the processes and principles for finding freedom from the fog of PTSD. This book can be used as a desk reference for the pastor or counselor as well as a self-help book for the person suffering with PTSD. I'm confident that Mike's book, *Tormented by PTSD?* will be your greatest resource concerning PTSD.

Ted Haggard
Senior Pastor, New Life Church
Colorado Springs, Colorado

Endorsements

It has been my pleasure to have Mike and Mary Petersen as good friends since the early '80s. In all that time I've never heard Mike complain or use any of his disabilities as an excuse. In my opinion, Mike has exemplified Paul's attitude of "I can do all things through Christ which strengthens me." He stands in stark contrast to multitudes of people today who allow life's slightest problems to hold them back. Mike preaches through his life in ways that words never could.

I thoroughly recommend this book, especially for anyone who has let some traumatic event sideline them. Mike's story and attitude will inspire you.

Andrew Wommack
Founder and President, Andrew Wommack Ministries Inc.
Colorado Springs, Colorado

No one knows the devastating effects war can have on a person's life like someone who has "been there". Mike Petersen has not only experienced the trauma of war, but shares how he faced life altered by both physical and emotional battlefield injuries. His story is one of incredible obstacles, but also of incredible courage and love. This story is not based merely on textbook knowledge, but on living life to the fullest everyday. His life has been a great inspiration to me personally and I believe that hearing Mike candidly share what has made the difference in his life will bring inspiration to all that read this book.

Joe Laughlin
Senior Pastor, Victory Church
Omaha, Nebraska

I have known Mike and Mary Petersen since March of 2001 when my family moved to Colorado Springs to start Charis Christian Center. Mike and Mary have been a tremendous blessing to the church and my family. I appreciate their faithfulness and steadfastness. Mike is one of the happiest people I know, which is a tremendous testimony considering the physical challenges that he faces.

Mike came to work for me as my personal assistant in October of 2004. He is very consistent. His work ethic is beyond that of most people in major leadership roles. I have observed him counseling and ministering to people in many trying situations. I have found that he is always positive and gives great advice to those who are in need. Mike's counsel in *Tormented by PTSD?* is something that he has personally experienced and has helped many others to accomplish. This is not a book of hypothesis, but a book of proven principles that have worked for Mike and many of those whom he has counseled.

Lawson Perdue,
Senior Pastor, Charis Christian Center
Colorado Springs, Colorado

Introduction

My desire to write this book was born out of a deep desire to help soldiers/veterans and their families overcome combat-related trauma, and Post-Traumatic Stress Disorder (PTSD), a disabling psychological condition resulting from a traumatic event. Our brave heroes are being told that there is no cure for this; that they will have to live with this the rest of their lives, but that they can learn to "cope." I, personally, know this is not true. Friends, *God*, and *He alone*, has the answer to all of our affliction and distress. It's His desire and will for you and your loved ones to be healed, delivered, and made free. It's mine too. I want to show you what he has shown me...the way out!

War is not only difficult for the military person but it is equally stressful on the family members back home. War is war, whether it is WWI, WWII, Korea, Vietnam, Persian Gulf, Afghanistan, Iraq, etc. Soldiers can be trained for war, but they are never totally prepared for what they will encounter. War is an ugly, ugly thing, very traumatizing to the soul. The mental pain and anguish of its memories can be excruciating, almost more than one can bear. The returning soldiers experience mental torment and emotional upheavals, (fear, shame, guilt, anger, grief, sorrow, loneliness, etc.) resulting from things they heard, things they saw, things they felt, things they tasted, things they smelled, and even participated in during their combat experience. Their memories of the war come back to haunt them day after day, night after night, and for some, even year after year. The majority of them do not have any idea what to do about all these thoughts and feelings. They continue in their "unshared," "quiet" misery, slowly dying inside, and making life miserable for most everyone around them, most of all, themselves. They stuff it, deny it, and ignore it, and hope that the nightmares, the

13

outbursts of anger, the "pushing away" of loved ones, the isolation, the sleeplessness, loneliness, depression and/or anxiety will all just "go away." Unfortunately, the closest family members take the biggest brunt of all this, but it is certainly not limited to just family members. Unchecked and undealt with negative emotions that go on year after year begin to take their toll on the minds, emotions, and even bodies of these wounded soldiers. They spend their life on anti-depression/anxiety drugs with all their side effects, and are still not well. Some end up in mental wards. Some end up suicidal and most with a myriad of chronic ailments and diseases, stemmed from the state of their souls. Proverbs 14:30 says, "A sound heart is the life of the flesh: but envy the rottenness of the bones." Over fifty-eight thousand American soldiers died in Vietnam. Regretfully, a much higher number have committed suicide. The actual numbers of these incidences vary from study to study. I recently heard a report on television that the Veterans Administration (VA) is expecting three times as many veterans from the war in Iraq to suffer from PTSD as their former comrades, the Vietnam veteran. My prayer is that the soldiers/veterans who are currently living in this kind of despair and hopelessness from hell will be freed from their "prison," and no longer feel the need to end their lives. I want to see the number of those turning to drugs and alcohol to numb the pain of the war be a thing of the past. I want to see relationships restored and these "heroes" experience the freedom that has already been bought and paid for by and through Jesus Christ. It is my hope that this book will enlighten its readers, deal with any unanswered questions regarding their combat experience, and help them to see that life can be good for them once again. They can receive genuine freedom from all that destroys, and live a life abundantly filled with God's love, peace and joy.

I have included a brief background history of myself. It is not my intention to dwell on my childhood or Vietnam experience, but rather after Vietnam, and how I obtained freedom from the mental anguish and negative emotions that controlled me, after my return home from war. Although I was never officially diagnosed with

PTSD, myself, I most definitely struggled with many negative emotions after Vietnam. They were and would have destroyed me, my wife and my children had I not found out how to master them instead of them mastering me. And over the past thirty-three years I have seen many veterans suffering from PTSD. It has hindered their ability to live strong, healthy, productive lives and maintain good strong family relationships. The struggle with PTSD symptomology (depression, anxiety, isolation, flashbacks, substance abuse, relationship issues, etc.) oftentimes leads to separation or divorce. I have also noticed an increased number of Christians suffering from various "psychological disorders." Brothers and sisters, any thing less than a life filled with genuine heart peace and joy is a life lived far below what Jesus Christ purchased for us at Calvary with His own blood. In John 10:10, Jesus said, "The thief cometh not, but for to steal, and to kill, and to destroy: I am come that they might have life, and that they might have it more abundantly." He also declared, "The Spirit of the Lord is upon me, because he hath anointed me to preach the gospel to the poor; he hath sent me to heal the brokenhearted, to preach deliverance to the captives and recovering of sight to the blind, to set at liberty them that are bruised, to preach the acceptable year of the Lord." (Luke 4:18–19). Isaiah 53, verses 4a and 5 says, "Surely he hath borne our grief, and carried our sorrows…But he was wounded for our transgressions, he was bruised for our iniquities: the chastisement of our peace was upon him: and with his stripes we are healed."

This book will deal with combat-related trauma, and the way to overcome it from a Biblical perspective. My emphasis will be on developing an intimate relationship with the Lord, the meditation of His Word, and the power of the Holy Spirit to do His miraculous workings in your life. I really hope to help you understand the importance and significance of a life surrendered completely to God. I pray that God would grant you a spirit of wisdom and revelation, open the eyes of your understanding, and flood your heart with light, and that you would know the truth and the truth would make you free.

I encourage you to pray this prayer before continuing. "Heavenly

Father, I thank You for your Word. I believe your Word is true and that You have sent the Holy Spirit to lead, guide, and teach me. Holy Spirit, I yield myself to You and ask that You reveal God's love and deliverance to me. Father, You are not a respecter of persons and I expect to receive your Word. Faith comes from hearing and hearing by the Word of God. I thank You, now, for the Word and receive my deliverance by faith, in Jesus name. Amen.

Chapter One: Childhood/Military

I was born and raised in a rural farming community in southwest Iowa. During my childhood we moved a couple of times for a fresh start, but it was never the answer. My parents divorced when I was a freshman in high school. At 14 years of age, I was forced to decide with whom I would live with. This was a hard time for me. I loved both of my parents. This is a decision that no child should ever have to make, but in our society, has become an every day occurrence. My sister and I chose to live with our father because we could remain around our friends. It was at this time, everything I had been accustomed to was uprooted, and I had to acquire a whole new outlook on life. My friends knew of the divorce but it was never spoken of and they always included me. Like most "baby-boomers," Godly principles were a part of growing up in a small farming community. Neighbors helped each other on a regular basis and socialized often together. This atmosphere helped strengthen the values and beliefs most of us had learned at home. I established friends in the community by the time I was four, and kept them all the way through grade and high school, sports, and church. Culture, demographics, and ethnicity certainly play their part to influence a person's values and beliefs.

It was also during my high school years that the Vietnam War was beginning to escalate. At first it was just something one watched on television, but then it came close to home. Alumni and friends were killed and other friends were being drafted. Most young men graduating in the sixties and seventies had military time and Vietnam ahead of them. By the time I graduated in 1967, three of my friends had already been killed and others were serving. I graduated at seventeen, worked the farms and on the railroad for two years, and then was drafted at nineteen into the United States Army in May of

1969. I trained at Fort Polk, Louisiana, both boot camp and AIT (Advanced Individual Training), with a MOS (Military Occupational Specialty) of 11B10 or infantry. It was during this training that I became very aware of my new friends, who became my new family. I understood they would be protecting me and I would be protecting them. I received orders for Vietnam, spent Christmas of '69 at home with a friend, who was home on leave also. The holiday itself did not mean anything to me. There was no family Christmas dinner, no gift exchange, no laughter, no joy. While on leave, I heard that another friend was seriously injured in Vietnam and expected home at any time. This wasn't news I wanted to hear just prior to my leaving for Vietnam. Two nights before leaving home I was sitting in a bar playing the old song, "Green Green Grass of Home." The more I listened to it, the more convinced I became that I probably would not come home from Vietnam alive. I began to imagine my own casket draped with a flag as my body was brought back to the United States. Singing and meditating on that song was planting a seed of death in me.

I reported in at Fort Lewis on January 2, 1970. While in processing, I made new friends. I began to question as many soldiers returning from Vietnam as I could, and suddenly new thoughts of returning home alive flooded my mind. The day finally arrived and we boarded an airliner with Vietnam as our final destination. Everyone on board tried to maintain composure and relax anyway we could during the flight, mine being three handed cribbage. As the plane descended, the captain's voice came over the intercom announcing that the airstrip was rocketed and we would circle until it was clear to land. The landing was successful. They shuffled us quickly off the plane, serviced it, and quickly took off with those headed home.

I instantly realized that my life had just made a drastic change. The smell, heat, and military compound reminded me of the stories told by returning soldiers. While waiting for duty assignment, I made new acquaintances. We were all silent, but thinking the same thing...wondering which of us would survive our tour. I can remember a large map of South Vietnam with the location of each military division. The orientation personnel told us what we could expect if assigned to a particular division (NVA, VC, booby-traps, delta area, highlands area, etc). I pointed to the map and told the soldier next to me that I would be assigned to the area with more VC and booby-traps (self-fulfilling prophecy). The day finally came when I was assigned to the Americal Division and flown to Chu Lai reception center. It was during this time that I met three GIs, with whom I had served with at Fort Benning, Georgia, and we had a good visit. A couple of days later we parted company and each received our individual orders for different units. I was assigned to the 11th Americal Division, 4/21 Co A, and flown to LZ (landing zone) Bronco, located at Duc Pho, (exactly the area pointed out on the map). The first night I pulled bunker guard with an African-American brother ready to return to the U.S. He had so many unanswered questions regarding racism back home, and wondered what he would encounter after being gone a year. I honestly told him, "I have no idea because I come from a small rural farming community in the Midwest." I couldn't believe that he had survived Vietnam and voiced a fear of returning home.

While at Bronco I met other new replacements and we all waited for company assignments. The day finally came and we were sent to our respective companies. We hoped to see each other on our return home, one year later. Three others and myself were taken to LZ Charley Brown, where three of us were assigned to the 3rd platoon. Our new CO (Commanding Officer) greeted us and gave us the standard military "pep talk." He explained that our platoon was building bunkers on LZ Debbie and we would be transported there the next day. Our names were promptly put on the bunker guard list and we were assigned to a bunker on the peninsula overlooking the inlet and village. I can remember thinking, "Vietnam is supposed to be hot. Why am I so cold with a long sleeve jungle fatigue shirt on?" Even so, I survived the first night, and I realized quickly that a new sleeping pattern was being groomed in me. The next morning as we waited for transport, I heard a shot and dirt kicked up approximately two feet on my right. The CO arrived and asked, "Where did that shot come from?" I pointed toward an APC (armored personnel carrier) ready to leave on road security. The CO walked up to the track searching for the GI that held the rifle whose barrel was warm and quickly grabbed him off the track. Suddenly it dawned on me that I had nearly been shot by one of our own before reaching my platoon...my first brush with death. This incident was resolved with a good lecture on gun safety. We were then transported to LZ Debbie where we met the members of the 3rd platoon. Immediately after introducing ourselves, they asked, "What is your nickname?"

I replied, "Pete," and the others followed with their nicknames. Instantly, we were all called by nickname only. This is the reason that many veterans can't remember the names of those killed or wounded who served with them.

Our platoon remained on LZ Debbie approximately one month after I arrived, building bunkers, RPG (rocket propelled grenade) screens, and pulling bunker guard. We were soon pulled from LZ Debbie and sent to Gilligan's Island, previously occupied by the Navy. While at Gilligan's Island we performed village security, pulled daily patrols, road security, and took turns pulling ambushes. On our first real patrol, we were choppered back into the mountains, and would patrol the area on our return, working with a dog and handler. We were about to enter the rice bowl (rice patties), when the dog smelled a booby-trap and alerted the handler. The handler began checking the area, when an explosion echoed loudly in our ears, followed by the cry for a medic. The handler had forgotten to reward the dog, leash him, and move him back away from the booby-trapped area before exploration. The dog had tripped the booby-trap when wagging its tail for a treat. The dog and handler were killed immediately, and two of our guys received shrapnel. As the med-evac was called, my mind was instantly flooded with thoughts of loading a dead person on the chopper. I couldn't believe this was happening on my first patrol. I gave a soft sigh of relief when the Lt. (lieutenant) told me to pull security, since I carried the M-60 machine gun. The chopper was quickly loaded with the dead and the wounded. The evacuation completed, we proceeded down the trail past the booby-trapped area. As I rounded a small bend in the trail, without warning, the dead dog loomed into view. I saw the dead dog and bloody booby-trapped area. It was a solemn ending to my first patrol and I quickly realized that nothing was predictable. Our company continued these types of operations for a couple of months and we grew accustomed to seeing friends injured or killed by either booby-traps or ambushes. The GIs, including me, became seasoned, revengeful, and waited for an opportunity to strike back. Then one evening as we prepared for guard duty, our CO told us that one of our sister companies had hit a daisy chain (a series of booby-traps using a single trip wire), designed to kill or maim a large number of people. The daisy chain had done exactly what it was designed to do. The company was instantly reduced to one-half its size. The remainder of this company would now be assigned to village pacification until their company numbers increased. Our company would replace its rotation off LZ Debbie.

The Vietnamese soldier was very crafty and oftentimes used our unexploded rounds against us. They would study our perimeters, trails we took, and take advantage of anything that appeared routine. The daisy chain booby-trap was retaliation against this company, who had been mutilating the dead bodies of the VC (Viet Cong). Many veterans still carry shame and guilt today for actions taken just like these. This booby-trap killed one of the replacements I had met at LZ Bronco during company assignment and was now the second replacement killed in the first four months.

Our company moved to LZ Debbie and immediately started a rotation cycle of two weeks in the field and one-week on the LZ. While in the field, we would search for the enemy by day, and pull ambushes at night. The missions became a game of "cat and mouse" and competition between platoons as to who got the most kills. The platoon with the most kills was rewarded with the bunkers closest to the mess hall and hot showers while on LZ Debbie. This added incentive stepped up our reasons for revengeful killing. We were determined to "redeem" every American soldier the Viet Cong and

NVA had killed or wounded. It got so intense my friends and I began taking risks by volunteering for special assignments, with the hope of finding "Charley" (VC/Viet Cong or NVA/North Vietnamese Army) and getting "another notch on our gun." We would look forward to our turn on LZ Debbie, even though bunker guard, road security, and short patrols were routine.

LZ Debbie provided a time to write letters and receive those "care packages" from back home. The care packages were a welcomed commodity and shared by everyone. We tried to relax, but found road security to be very hazardous at times. We frequently saw civilians and comrades wounded or killed by booby-traps planted by the VC. One sunny morning our platoon was dropped off by the track unit for a routine road security mission. That day, our squad leader/pointman decided to use the back trail on the hill, overlooking the rice bowl and highway. We hadn't been setup more than ten minutes when an explosion rang out on the front trail. Some of us ran toward the explosion, while the others stayed on the hill, watching for enemy activity. As they approached the location, they found two young Vietnamese soda girls, (young girls selling soda to the GI) injured by the blast. Our acting medic quickly went to work and our radioman called for a "dust-off." We heard later, that one of the young girls had died from the wounds. We returned to the LZ that evening and questioned members of the other squads who had previously pulled road security in that area. We found out that these squads had been using the front trail on a regular basis. It was the decision to use the back trail, by our pointman, that had kept us from a mishap. We started searching villages for people loyal to the VC and confiscated the rice caches. We found often, that villagers would be friends during the day and foes at night. They were in the middle and oftentimes didn't know which way to turn. They frequently played both sides. These villagers could be men, women, young and old, teens, and/or young children. This strongly influenced our ability to trust. We oftentimes found it safer in the mountains away from the villages and their VC activities.

As I counted down the days on my tour, the number of my friends

killed or wounded mounted. I wrote my cousin about the guys being lost to booby-traps, and told her, "You never know who might be next." Less than one month later, on August 24, 1970, seven of us left our temporary base camp on a routine patrol and OP (observation post). A couple of days earlier, one of our platoon members had hit a booby-trap on their return from an OP. As we prepared to leave the perimeter, I knelt down to remove the trip flare, and placed my helmet on the ground. I folded back the concertina wire, allowing us an exit route. When the patrol filed out, I replaced the wire, but forgot to pick up my helmet. We were to patrol out, pull the OP, and return by a different route. We decided the machine gun wasn't necessary since the OP wasn't that far from the perimeter, so instead, I carried the radio on the way out. I volunteered to walk point on our return. After all, it was a routine patrol and we were headed back in. I remember jumping an irrigation ditch, when our squad leader called for a short break with the perimeter in sight. Our break was soon over. We saddled up and started to move. I took one step. There was a loud explosion. I had hit a buried landmine. I remember the sensation of falling into a large hole, rebounding, and falling again. As the sensation of falling occurred, I saw a bright light, which disappeared, after I finally came to rest. I was lying flat on my back, facing the opposite direction, and maneuvered myself with my elbows away from what I thought was a blown cavern. I immediately thanked God that I was alive, called for the medic, and noticed my friend calling for the med-evac. The medic was new and had just joined us prior to the patrol..."Welcome to Vietnam." I can remember a seasoned medic, our Lt., and other members of my platoon running from the perimeter to help. The urge to explore the injuries was over-whelming, but my arms wouldn't move. I asked the medic, "Why can't I move my arms?"

He barked, "They are broken. Now lay still!" He worked frantically, while a friend knelt by me, talking about home, fishing together, and reassuring me that everything was okay. This was all standard procedure to prevent the wounded soldier from going into shock. I heard the sound of a chopper approaching, and knew the "dust-off" was near. My mind kept telling me that everything would be okay once the med-evac arrived, but little did I know that this ride could have been fatal. I closed my eyes to prevent dirt blowing in them, as the chopper landed. I was placed on the floor behind the co-pilot, next to my squad leader, who was also wounded. While airborne, I felt my throat and mouth filling with blood, and I began choking. I managed to clear my throat, but it immediately started to fill with blood again…a result of the internal injuries. These internal injuries would later leave extensive scarring throughout my mid-section. As gruesome as this sounds, I looked like someone had taken a knife and split me open from the rib cage to the groin. I managed to inch my way to the co-pilot's seat and turn on my side using his seat back as support. This allowed the blood to drain from my throat, and not choke me while in flight. The med-evac was approximately fifteen minutes. I was met by a triage team. They questioned me about notifying family. The doctors asked my name and service number in order to determine coherence. They were amazed at my alertness. The field medic had given me no morphine. In retrospect, this was probably a good thing (the hand of God), because I would not have been coherent enough on the chopper to turn on my side, and keep from choking. I would have drowned in my own blood and died. I was then rushed to surgery and don't remember how many days I lost. I remember being awakened by a choking sensation and wondering how to get someone's attention. I frantically used my bandaged forearms and hit the bed rails. A nurse ran to my assistance. I pointed to my mouth. She noticed that my tongue had come out from under the tongue suppressor. She repositioned it and I immediately went back to sleep. When I awoke again, I asked a nurse for something to drink, but was told I couldn't have anything. She told me that I was being transferred to Japan and left my bedside. However, she returned shortly and much to my relief, thrust a straw in my mouth, and told me to drink quickly. It was lemonade she had received in a care package herself. She walked alongside the stretcher, as I was loaded on the aircraft destined for Japan. I never knew her name and don't to this day, but thank God for the "Florence

Nightingales" who serve during wartime.

I arrived in Japan with the other wounded, and talked to the ambulance driver while en route to the hospital. His assistant asked how I had been injured, so I proceeded to tell him. I explained how fortunate I was to have my legs, since everyone I knew who had hit a mine had lost their legs. I hadn't been told of the loss and there was a continual sensation of having legs. It simply felt like they were asleep. At this point I heard the driver hit his assistant. He stopped talking and I still had no clue as to the loss of my legs.

My stay at the hospital in Japan brought many challenges. I arrived at the hospital and was introduced to a surgeon. He asked me what I planned on doing (job-wise) when I got home.

I emphatically said, "I'm going back to work on the railroad." There was utter silence. You could hear a pin drop.

The doctor took a long breath and asked, "Hasn't anyone told you about the loss of your legs?"

I replied, "No..." Nothing more was said regarding my injuries. He left my bedside telling me he would see me in surgery the next morning. It was very late at night. I was exhausted and fell asleep.

I went through the surgery, lost more time, and awoke with a Red Cross volunteer sitting at my bedside. When she realized I was awake, she asked, "Is there a family member we could fly here?"

I replied, "No, I'll be home before long." Years later, I found out the Red Cross only asked that question to those whom they didn't think were going to make it. I assume, but don't have absolute knowledge, that I must have gone into shock after hearing I had lost my legs. Both legs had been blown off above the knee, the right just below the hip. A few days after surgery, I was started on whirlpool treatments. I couldn't balance myself, so an orderly was always present to hold me upright or place a crutch across the whirlpool tub for me to drape my arms over. Afterwards, I was always given the option to stay in the therapy area and visit, or go back to the ward. I usually chose to remain and talk to the orderlies, rather than returning to the ward. They made me laugh and often gave me a soda. I looked forward to and enjoyed this time every day.

Then the day came for some real food. It was my first real meal since being injured and within a few hours I threw it up. Everyone came scrambling to my aid. The next thing I knew there was a tube being shoved down my throat. The tube was uncomfortable and I removed it after the nurses left my bedside. The nurse returned later, saw the tube lying next to me, and asked, "Who removed the tube?"

I replied "I did," and she immediately inserted it again. The removal and insertion of the tube was done two more times before I gave up and left it alone. This stubborn determination was undoubtedly a definite asset in helping me recover. I was a fighter and never gave up easily. Little did I know I also had a Grandma and many others back home praying for me. No doubt, God had heard and was restoring health to me. These are all things I would come to know later after I received the Lord Jesus myself. While in Japan my squad leader came by, patted my shoulder, and said that he was being shipped home, but he wanted to see me first. I asked how bad his injury was and he said it wasn't bad, although he was using a cane. I told him goodbye and never saw or heard from him again.

My first encounter with a combat-related nightmare also came while I was in Japan. I woke up screaming, handing to the nurse, what I thought was a live grenade, and telling her to throw it...quick! As soon as the nurse touched my hands, I fell back asleep. I sometimes think of the treatment I received at the Japan hospital and those who worked there. Outside of the Lord, I don't know how the medical and therapy staff maintained their sanity, seeing the multitude of wounded and those who died in the hospital. I used to watch *M.A.S.H.* once in awhile. I've often thought it must be pretty realistic, how humor and alcohol became a way of escape for them. I wish I could personally thank every person on the medical teams who contributed to keeping me alive.

I left Japan after a few weeks, and while en route to Walter Reed, we were only scheduled to land in Alaska to refuel. However, during the flight, my condition became very unstable, so they left me there at the Air Force Hospital. I had spent most of the time in Vietnam and Japan sedated, and slept much of that time, but at the Air Force Hospital, I was becoming more alert and staying awake for longer periods of time. It was at this time that I decided to explore my injuries. I touched what was left of my left leg. I became nauseated. I made the decision at that time not to do any more exploration on my own. My condition was soon stabilized, and I was flown to an over-crowded Walter Reed Army Hospital, in Washington, D.C. The ward was so full that they left me in the hallway and gave me a small bell to ding if I needed help. The first night I was there, I woke up from a nightmare, hit the bell, and got no response. Eventually, a nurse showed up, panting and out of breath. She quickly apologized for not remembering my temporary location. She had run the whole ward looking for the bell, but when she couldn't find it, thought she might be hearing things. It was very late and I knew she was exhausted. She heard it again and had remembered my hallway location. She brought me some water and talked to me until I was able to fall asleep again. The nursing staff was always ready to listen. They provided the soldiers, including me, with so much encouragement and support.

At Walter Reed I had a couple more surgeries and soon found out about another result of the explosion. One afternoon, I was awakened when someone bumped my bed and started groping for my hand. He found my hand, shook it, and introduced himself as Mr. Williams from the Blinded Veterans Association (BVA). This was my first news as to the seriousness of the injury to my eyes. Although I was aware of the routine eye-patch changes and drops, I never dreamed I wouldn't see again. I don't know whether it was poor bedside manner, or, that the medical staff didn't have the heart to tell me. This day was very rough for me, and the staff and other patients visited me often. I had already been struggling and still trying to adjust to the loss of both my legs above the knee, but this was the ultimate blow for me. A thousand thoughts were going through my mind. I felt that a man with no legs was only half a man, but a man with no eyes was no man at all. I didn't know how I would ever be able to do *anything*, let alone my dreams…dreams of going back to the railroad, working my own farm, hunting, and even becoming a forest ranger (something I had dreamed of being since I was a kid). I was only twenty years old. My whole life had been ahead of me, but everything stopped. Now it seemed it had ended.

The time at Walter Reed was used for debriefing, reintegration into society, as well as gaining strength; (my weight was only 65 pounds). Reintegration was done through visitations with family, celebrities, fellow veterans, and staff members. My mom and step-dad arrived at Walter Reed just a few days after me, and stayed for a week. My mom kissed me on the cheek with tears streaming down her face and quickly left my bedside. She regained her composure, came back to me and spent the rest of the week talking about things back home. I celebrated my twenty-first birthday at Walter Reed with my dad, the staff, and patients. Debriefing was taking place, as many of us patients would talk about our war experiences with each other. None of us realized just how important this was at the time. Stronger patients would oftentimes help the weaker ones. This is how I developed one very close friendship from there. I wasn't able to feed myself at first because both arms were bandaged from the elbow to the end of my fingertips. They were burned, broken, and had been ripped open from hurling shrapnel. Doug Deacon, another double amputee injured in Vietnam, would come and feed me first. He would return to his bed and eat his food cold. He and his family continually helped me with anything I needed (read my mail to me, filled out my menus, brought snacks, kept my family updated, etc.). This brings a scripture to my mind. "Greater love hath no man than this, that a man lay down his life for his friends." (John 15:13) This scripture is referring to God's love, His ultimate sacrifice of His life on the cross, but I strongly felt this kind of love from Doug. He was a clown, and a practical jokester, and played his share of pranks on me, which made us both laugh. However, when it came to serious situations, he sacrificed his own comfort for mine many times. He was always looking out for me. Many soldiers and veterans feel like all they have are each other. For this reason there is still a very strong camaraderie existing between most Vietnam veterans today. This book is dedicated to the memory of Doug, my closest friend on earth (next to Jesus and my wife, of course).

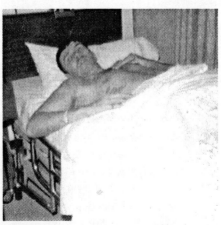

I was transferred from Walter Reed to the Veterans Administration Medical Center (VAMC) at Omaha, Nebraska, the week before Thanksgiving 1970. My sister and brother-in-law came that weekend from Des Moines, and made plans to take me home for Thanksgiving. Nurses instructed them on proper bandage changes (both legs were still open) and how to transfer me to and from the wheelchair. My brother-in-law, who had served in Vietnam a few years earlier, changed the wraps on a daily basis. It was good to be close to home and have other family members come for a visit. The pass was shortened when my brother-in-law noticed a discoloration of one leg. He called the hospital, described the discoloration, and was told to bring me back immediately. As soon as I arrived, an IV was started to fight the infection and afterward a couple of surgeries were scheduled. These new surgeries made it impossible to go on pass at Christmas, but in spite of all that I had the best Christmas ever. Are you wondering how could this be? After all, what is Christmas, when you are laying in a hospital bed, with no legs or eyesight, one royally messed up arm and hand, without family, Christmas trees, lights, music, presents, the traditional ham dinner, and old friends from home? But on December 22, 1970, a group of senior girls from Notre Dame Academy (an all-girls Catholic high school) visited the VA Hospital to spread Christmas cheer. Immediately after they left, I called my sister and told her that I was getting married (self-fulfilling prophecy again), but didn't know her name yet. The next day, two of the girls returned with a Christmas present. They continued coming every day over the holidays, bringing all the Christmas goodies they could think of. I was soon able to distinguish the difference between their voices, and gravitated toward the one I had phoned my sister about and believed I would marry. Because it was Christmas time, a nurse had hung mistletoe on the grab bar above my bed. On Christmas Eve I asked Mary if she would kiss me under the mistletoe. She told me no, but being the persistent fellow that I am, I coaxed her again a week later. On New Years Eve, 1970, we had our first kiss. Mary says, "It was love at first sight," but you could say, "It was love at first sound," for me! Mary would come to the hospital every day and escort me to physical therapy, where she would continually give me words of encouragement. This added encouragement made physical therapy much easier for me and gave me an incentive to get well faster. I began to recover rapidly and had a strong desire to be out of the hospital. It was during one of these physical therapy sessions that my rehab doctor took the liberty to talk with Mary. He advised her against any thoughts of marriage, since statistics showed that marriages to a disabled person usually end in divorce. Mary was very quiet as she took me back to my ward and I sensed she was troubled. As I questioned her, she told me what had transpired while I was in physical therapy. The next day, on my way to physical therapy, I stopped by the rehab doctor's office. I reminded him of his position as my rehab doctor…*only!* My personal life was none of his business. In retrospect, I believe he was probably genuinely concerned, as we were both so young, and had only known each other for such a short time before talking of marriage. However, this did not stop us. Our feelings for each other were too strong, and we really believed we had something very special between us. So, I met Mary's family on January 18, 1971, at her eighteenth birthday party. I liked them and they liked me. We spent time together every day and talked on the phone. We laughed a lot and got passes from the hospital for me so we could go out on dates. We enjoyed dinners together, movies, picnics, and "get-togethers" with Mary's parents, sisters, and brothers. Our relationship was growing stronger. I gave her a promise ring on Valentine's Day (1971) and asked her to marry me, presenting her with an engagement ring at her high school graduation (May 1971). People were skeptical and many wondered what Mary and I were thinking, but none of their doubts deterred us. Both sets of parents were for us, and we really believed our love for each other was much greater than the circumstances we faced, as all young couples do. Little did we know, how this love of ours would be severely tried, and that our own human, earthly love would not be enough to take us over. We would need a love much greater than ours…God's kind of love. Mary's parents had a standing family rule that all of the kids had to wait at least one year after graduation before getting married. One evening as we sat around the kitchen talking about wedding plans with her parents, aunt, and uncle, Mary's Uncle Frank looked at Mary's dad and said, "Come on, Willie Joe, let the kids get married early."

Mary's dad said, "Okay," and a wedding date of August 21, 1971, was set just three months after she graduated. The wedding ceremony took place just three days short of the one-year anniversary of my being injured. It was a wonderful day and just the beginning of our journey together. Proverbs 18:22 says "Whoso findeth a wife findeth a good thing, and obtaineth favour of the *Lord*." I've experienced the blessedness of this truth. Marriage is a wonderfully, good thing! Our marriage of thirty-four years (August 2005) has not been void of a few heartaches and trouble at times, but we've made it through each situation victoriously with God and His Word. Our marriage is a good thing!

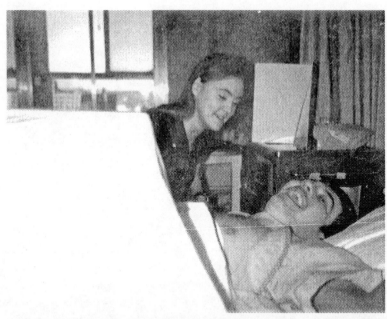

Chapter Two: Adjusting Time

The early years of marriage brought many trials adjusting to the disabilities and the memories of war. Our honeymoon brought the first trial and probably a big question in my lovely new bride's mind. Only four days into our honeymoon, a nightmare awakened me in stark terror, only to hear my wife's voice in the distance, but unable to answer. I lay there in a frozen state until I was able to talk, and whisper, "It was a nightmare and nothing else." Vietnam was a thing of the past, and my beautiful new bride didn't need to know the horrors of war. Most returning veterans aren't ready to discuss their combat experiences with anyone but another veteran. There is an existing trust issue and most don't believe a civilian will understand.

Honeymoon over, we moved into our first home together. It was difficult for me adapting to the wheelchair and being unable to see. I had been accustomed to hard work and recreation outdoors. I was forced to give up things I previously enjoyed (hunting and working the farms), but my wife freely gave up things she liked and enjoyed doing out of her love for me. The first months of marriage were dedicated to dealing with the multiple disabilities, (double amputee above knee, blind, limited use of one arm/hand, and miscellaneous other injuries) and getting to know each other more. I found myself frustrated, angry, and fearful much of the time. If someone upset me or didn't "do me right," in my opinion, I would give them a piece of my mind, usually using foul language. I had a constant feeling that everyone was "out to get me," and rip me off. We were living in a big city, and I lived in constant paranoia of a break-in, probably from being a country boy and my experiences in Vietnam. We immediately acquired our first dog; a fine German shepherd to "protect" me when Mary was gone. Mary spent most of these first years just trying to help me, keep me calm and happy, but always encouraging me and pushing me to do things on my own. We not only had our personal adjustments, but we were faced with adjusting to many structural barriers. The ability to freely maneuver a wheelchair in most surroundings in 1971 was difficult. Wheelchair access to most buildings was oftentimes limited but we didn't let this stop us. We learned as a team. I could ascend/descend stairs on my hands and bottom, and then jump back into the waiting wheelchair, which Mary would pickup and carry up or down the stairs to me. We had this down to a science. We always seemed to figure out a way for us to go and do anything we wanted to do, things that would have kept most wheelchair-bound people out.

Mary and I wanted to start a family immediately, but doctors had told us it was very probable that we would not be able to have children because of all the shrapnel I had taken. As tests were being performed to confirm this probability, the doctor asked, "What are your career plans?" I looked at him funny, as if to say, "In case you haven't noticed, I'm a double amputee and blind." He responded to me with, "Men have never made good house pets. You should consider at least a hobby." He sent me out of the office with some medicine, and said, "Maybe this will help." God was working and neither Mary nor I even knew Him yet. A few months later Mary was pregnant with our first child, a daughter born on my twenty-third birthday. What a birthday present! God is a *good* God! She was everything we had hoped and dreamed for. She was beautiful and perfect in every way. She was our joy and delight…and still is.

Doug Deacon (my friend from Walter Reed) and I had become very close. He was still very much a part of my life. He had a friend of the family, in Michigan, who was an eye doctor's nurse. She would review all the latest developments in eye research. She discovered a new surgery technique in 1974, called Doug, and he took the liberty of contacting the eye surgeon in Boston, Massachusetts. Doug called me and explained the new surgery technique to me. He said the surgeon wanted to see my records. The VA sent my records. The doctor and his colleagues reviewed them. I phoned and scheduled for an evaluation appointment. My wife, one year old daughter, mother-in-law and I flew to Boston in September 1974 to see the eye specialist. The first night in a strange city, sitting in our hotel room, I remembered a friend, Thomas Bernhardt Jr., better known as "Skip," whom I had served with in Vietnam, being from Boston. I had my wife search the phone directories. She found the listing. I called him, and after a short talk he said he would be right down. He brought his photo albums containing pictures of Vietnam for us to see. When he and his wife arrived and introductions were completed, he dropped the photo album in front of me on the bed. At this point I told him I couldn't see. He had no idea of the severity of my injuries because he was on leave when I was injured. I explained why we were there and he immediately took the next few days off work to escort us around. He went to the eye specialist with us and was a great comfort to Mary, as I not only met with the main eye specialist but each of his colleagues. The evaluation was completed. Surgery was scheduled. The doctors gave me a one in a hundred chance of improving the light perception in only one eye. Nothing could be done for the other eye that had severe damage. In the eye they were going to operate on, the retina had been detached. I would eventually lose what light perception I already had, so with nothing to lose I said yes to the surgery that would try to re-attach the retina. They scheduled my surgery for November 1974. Skip insisted that my wife, daughter, and mother-in-law stay at his place while I was in the hospital and the two weeks after my release from the hospital. Skip and his wife, Arlene, were so gracious to us. I hadn't seen him since Vietnam but they treated us like we were family. Skip showed Mary how to get to and from the hospital on the Boston subways. This was a big deal for a very young girl from the Midwest. They were just as good to my mother-in-law and our two-year-old daughter, Traci. Before leaving Boston they made sure we got in some sightseeing. They took us to the ocean, fine restaurants, and historical spots around Boston. They were such a blessing to us. It was sad to leave them. We are still good friends today. The surgery was a success. They were able to attach the retina. However, it only gave me a very minimal amount of more sight than I had. I was still considered legally blind. I could now read again with the aid of very high powered reading glasses, a bright light, and holding the printed page about one inch from my nose. I could play chess, see a deck of jumbo playing cards, which opened up a lot of card playing for me. I could even see outlines, movements, and shapes on television if I sat inches from it. This made watching television a little more enjoyable. I remembered what the doctor had said earlier about finding a hobby and decided to explore VA Vocational Rehab.

God blessed us with three more children during those first eight years of marriage, a total of three precious, beautiful daughters and one wonderful and handsome son; each one, so special, so unique, so intricately created by the hand of God. We treasured each of them, still not really realizing that it was *God* who had been so good and gracious to us. They are all our biggest blessing…by far, the most precious gifts God has bestowed on us.

Even though there were limitations, I still enjoyed an active part in my children's growing up. We had to make modifications at times. Mary tirelessly tried to keep my path in the house clear of toys, shoes, and things in general. The kids learned very young to "keep out of dad's path," but not always soon enough. I do remember wheeling over a few fingers of crawling babies. I fed our babies, feeling for their mouths with the finger next to the one that held the bottle or spoon. I changed diapers…ouch! I stuck myself more than once with their pins…never them. I thanked God the day "Pampers" came out. I dressed them…sometimes backwards, sometimes inside out, but their bodies were covered up. Mary became the "fashion inspector" every time before we left the house. At one time, we had a 3-year-old, a 10-month-old, and a newborn. Leaving the house was a sight! We taught Traci (the 3-year-old) to always hold on to the arm of the wheelchair and walk beside me. I sat Erin (our 10 month old) on what was left of my left leg, and sat Michael (the newborn) in his infant seat on what was left of my right leg. I held them tight. Mary would push and steer the wheelchair and off we'd go. They learned at a very young age to describe in detail things they wanted me to "see." They would also bring their "treasures" or new shoes to me to feel so I could "see" them. In a croquet game, the kids would tap the wires with their mallet to let me know where to aim my ball and hit it through. Sometimes I made it. Sometimes I didn't. They would tell me when to swing the bat for wiffle ball. I was still able to play. I enjoyed the times swinging the kids, playing wiffle ball, and even teaching them how to ride their bikes. I remember taking our oldest daughter out almost daily, in the nice weather, when she was around 2 years old, and tying her red wagon to the back of my wheelchair with a rope. I would pull her down our 300-foot driveway, turn around, and bring her back up. I put endless Christmas toys together, by feel, and even played with a few of them before retiring them under the Christmas tree. The kids never seemed to think their dad was "odd." They never seemed to look at me differently, even though it was obvious, I was. When our youngest daughter, Maggie, while in the third grade, wrote a story about me, one day, Mary and I received a phone call from her teacher. The teacher was very concerned because Maggie had never talked about or discussed her father's disabilities with her, but she had written about them in her story. She thought that Maggie, perhaps, needed counseling, because she had never brought up my disabilities before having to write this essay. We discussed it with Maggie. She told us she never thought about it until she went to write a story about me. She said she never thought about me being anything but her dad. All of our kids, now being grown up, say the same thing. I assume and suppose it is because they never knew it to be any other way. And, neither Mary nor I ever acted like anything was wrong. As a matter of fact, "quite contraire!" We just went about living life, and always figuring out a way to do just about anything, as a family, that any other family enjoyed. The kids just enjoyed being with me, and doing with me, what I could do, the way I could do it. I enjoyed them even more. Even though the disabilities created some limitations, I wasn't about to let it keep me from enjoying my children's childhood.... more of that "hardheadedness" of mine. I'm sure the kids missed out on a few things, but Mary and I always tried to make the best of every situation. We didn't believe in obstacles. We believed we could overcome just about anything. We played with our kids outside. We played with them inside. We picnicked, took vacations, went to movies, and played games. We had snowball fights in the winter, built snowmen, and took them ice skating the old-fashioned way, outside on a park pond. We went sledding and skiing. We flew kites in the spring, and had our share of "Easter egg hunts." We took them swimming and boating in the summers, and because Mary and I love and enjoy baseball; we often took them to Rockies baseball games, as they got older. There was never enough room for us all to sit in the "handicapped" section (they only sit 2), so we would purchase better seats down closer. I scooted on my bottom down to our row of seats, and back up, sometimes through popcorn, peanuts, and yes, even spilled pop and beer. I still do this if more than Mary and I go. In the fall, I helped Mary in the yard. We raked leaves into piles, so the kids could jump right in the middle of them, and then did it all over again the next year. Our kids enjoyed me being home all the time. Mary did, too. We didn't really know anything different. It's just the way it was. But, as time went on, I became unsettled, and discontent. I remembered the doctor's words spoken to me when we went to see if I would be able to give Mary the children she and I wanted so badly. Home was good, but it just wasn't quite enough.

It was during this time that I made a decision to go to a technical school, and received an Associate Degree in Auto-Mechanics, which I used solely for my hobby of car restoration, which I still enjoy today. I had contacted several mechanic shops about gainful employment, but they discouraged me from pursuing a career in auto mechanics because of the liability and safety issues. So, I purchased old cars and used what I had learned, to restore them, in my own home garage. This gave me something "manly" to do; however, this wasn't enough either, for the male ego. I was still helping Mary around the house, doing dishes, cleaning up and handy-man work, that was within my reach. I even cooked when Mary was unable, and kept our children often, while Mary ran errands, or went on an outing somewhere. I seemed to be able to figure out how to do just about anything from landscaping work, to working on our car, to housework. As any blind person, I would do it all by feel. Even so, Mary and I were beside ourselves! We thought we had the "tiger-by-the-tail." But I wasn't totally satisfied or fulfilled. I wanted a real job and to be recognized as a part of the working world. I wanted to leave our home, and go to work. I saw the opportunity to go into training for a VA Prosthetic Representative, so I took it. I finished the training, but was denied employment due to sight limitation. Once again, the disability stood in the way of employment and thoughts of never being productive in the working world, away from my home, entered my mind.

The adjustment to the disabilities, marriage, and a feeling of no worth to society began to weigh on me. I knew I was loved, admired and respected by family and close friends. I knew I had accomplished so much, and that it was enough to keep me busy and happy at home, but that desire to contribute back into society was always there, underlying, gnawing at me all the time. Before military service I had been very productive on the railroad, in construction, and on the farm, and I wanted and needed to be that productive again. I didn't spend my days in depression. I was much too happy with Mary, the kids, other family and friends for that. But I just needed more. I give credit to my wife's stamina throughout our marriage. I dealt with many years of anger and frustration because the disabilities (mainly the impaired vision) limited my activity, and most of all, seemed to be the main factor in stopping me from getting what I called, a "real" job. I knew many other veterans in wheelchairs who were still able to drive, play sports, have gainful employment, etc. And even though I could do more than I ever thought I would be able to, there was still so much I wanted to do, but couldn't...or couldn't seem to find the way. Like many veterans, I would have an occasional down day. I had thoughts that Mary and the kids would be better off without me. I was ready to run, but because my wife had a strong commitment, she always encouraged open communication. She would often say, "You're not going anywhere. We made vows to God and each other that we would love each other and not depart from each other until death. You're not dead, and neither am I. Now, get in here, and let's talk." Mary is usually very understanding, and has a gentleness about her, but when she means business, you listen! And so I would...with a little fight. Mary can rise up "as bold as a lion," at the first thought that the devil is trying to rob her. We would get it straightened out and off we would go again. Mary knew how much I missed being on the farm, so every summer we would pack the car and head to my mother's farm for a few days so I could enjoy the smells and sounds of the country again.

In 1978, Mary began questioning what life was all about. She began to realize that with all we had accomplished and were enjoying, she wasn't satisfied either. There was something missing, but she had no idea what. It was during this time of questioning that she heard and received God's good news, the gospel of Jesus Christ. She invited Jesus Christ to come into her heart as the Lord (Master) and Savior of her life. I could not deny the changes I saw in her...mostly such great peace and contentment, and her love toward me seemed to get even sweeter. She quit reacting to my displays of anger, and would either say nothing, or speak back to me in a soft and gentle manner. She made me hungrier and hungrier to understand what had happened to her. I began asking her questions. One night we were at a movie and right before the movie started, she told me she had found Jesus. I responded sarcastically, "Where was He hiding? I didn't know He was lost." But, it was only one year later while questioning God myself about a friend's death, while watching a television evangelist one Sunday morning, that I, too, received the Lord, and gave Him my life. *Wow!* We were so excited! We had been born again! "Jesus answered and said unto him, Verily, verily, I say unto thee, Except a man be born again, he cannot see the kingdom of God. Nicodemus sayeth unto him, How can a man be born when he is old? Can he enter the second time into his mother's womb, and be born? Jesus answered, Verily, verily, I say unto thee, Except a man be born of water and of the Spirit, he cannot enter into the kingdom of God. That which is born of the flesh is flesh; and that which is born of the Spirit is spirit. Marvel not that I said unto thee, Ye must be born again. The wind bloweth where it lifteth, and thou hearest the sound thereof, but canst not tell whence it cometh, and whither it goest; so is every one that is born of the Spirit." (John 3:3–8) All things had become new! We *knew* we were two different people…still Mike and Mary Petersen, but something had changed! The nightmares that I still had occasionally, stopped immediately. Our desires began to change. Slowly and little by little, our taste in music changed. We went from loving Elvis, the Beatles, John Denver and rock and roll, to contemporary music about the Lord. No one told us we had to do this. We were just so hungry for God! We couldn't seem to get enough of Him or His Word. We found ourselves watching Christian television and listening to Christian radio. The more we fell in love with Jesus, the more we began to change…in every area. There didn't seem to be an area He wasn't touching. However, as we kept walking with Him and growing in Him, we became very aware of things in our life that didn't just disappear, instantly. Although anger outbursts had begun to subside, I still found myself frustrated, angry, still "cussing," still afraid, still insecure, and still unable to control these emotions at times. We had joined a Bible believing and preaching church, and were hearing the Word of God about salvation, and that He was coming again to get us. It was great! We were finally beginning to understand what salvation was all about, what did indeed happen to us, and the teaching on the Second Coming of Jesus really excited us and stirred our hearts. We knew we were saved. "That if thou shalt confess with thy mouth the Lord Jesus, and shalt believe in thine heart that God hath raised him from the dead, thou shalt be saved. For with the heart man believeth unto righteousness; and with the mouth confession is made unto salvation." (Romans 10:9, 10) We knew we were going to heaven. "The Spirit itself beareth witness with our spirit, that we are the children of God: And if children, then heirs; heirs of God, and joint-heirs with Christ…" (Romans 8:16, 17a) We knew Jesus was coming again. "For as the lightning cometh out of the east, and shineth even unto the west; so shall also the coming of the Son of man be." (Matthew 24:27) We had already, by this time, started telling others about what had happened to us, and giving the gospel to them. God was bringing hungry and thirsty people to us, and we had the wonderful opportunity of leading many of them to the Lord. But, while all this was happening, we were struggling in our own lives with our own individual issues. Mary and I both so desperately wanted to know how to live the abundant life we read about in the Bible, here on earth. This does not mean a life void of persecution or trials, but a life of victory in them, through them, and over them. "…I am come that they might have life, and that they might have it more abundantly" (John 10:10b). We thought, surely, God could set us free from any residual anger, shame, guilt, fear, depression, anxiety, loneliness, insecurity, and instability that still seemed to "hang on," from our "old life." Well, we not only found out we could walk in freedom from all these things, but we could be free from *all* that the curse had brought on this earth through Adam's sin. This included sickness and disease and financial debt. There was a place in God, where the things of this world had no hold on us. One day, turning on Christian radio, I heard a man of God teaching things I had never heard yet in the 2–3 years I had been saved. I almost couldn't believe what I was hearing, but there was a witness deep in my heart, that it was right. I began to hear exactly what had happened to me when I got born again. I began to hear who I was in Christ, and just what He did for me at the cross of Calvary. I found out I was a three part being, and that my spirit had been reborn, but I still had a soul and a body to deal with on this earth, for as long as I am here. I saw that God cannot lie, and that His Word is true, the only real Truth. I heard him teach on scriptures saying that I could be transformed by the renewing of my mind. "I beseech thee brethren by the mercies of God that you present your bodies a living sacrifice, holy, acceptable to God, which is your reasonable service. And do not be conformed to this world but be transformed by the renewing of your mind, that you may prove what is that good and acceptable and perfect will of God (Romans 12:1, 2). I was stunned when I saw in Proverbs 23:7a, that "For as he thinketh in his heart, so is he…" These scriptures really caught my attention. For the first time, I began to realize I needed to change my thinking. If only I could change the way I think, just maybe all the negative emotions that still seemed to control my life, would be a thing of the past. I mentioned previously that the nightmares stopped immediately, but the anger towards my limitations due to the disability remained. I decided to take God at His Word. Either it was true, or it wasn't. I began to spend hours a day renewing my mind in the Word of God. I fasted. I prayed. I started studying the Word like I had never studied it before. I dug. I delved. I searched. With every minute, the excitement grew. Could it be true? Could I really be different? Mary and I drove hours across the country to hear the Word of God preached and taught. We were like two baby birds with our beaks wide open, waiting for the worm. We listened to men of God teach us these powerful truths. And God filled us, and filled us, and filled us! "Blessed are they who hunger and thirst after righteousness: for they shall be filled." (Matthew 5:6) I found specific scriptures that ministered to me, on the love and mercy of God, fear, forgiveness, and who I was *now* in Christ Jesus. Little by little I found myself less and less frustrated, angry, and fearful.

The first scriptures that really struck me and have become among my favorites are, "Brethren, I count not myself to have apprehended: but this one thing I do, forgetting those things which are behind, and reaching forth unto those things which are before, I press toward the mark for the prize of the high calling of God in Christ Jesus." (Philippians 3:13, 14). I received revelation of these two scriptures and was finally able to put Vietnam in the past. Little did I know how God would use me in the future to minister this very truth to numbers of Vietnam veterans. Right after we both got born again, Mary told me numerous times that God would use me one day in this way. "No way!" was my emphatic answer. I knew so many Vietnam veterans that were whiners, complainers, "cry babies," in my opinion. I wanted nothing to do with most of them. I had no idea, the love and compassion God was about to drop in my heart for them.

About this time, as we kept listening to the teacher on Christian radio that brought us the truths I will be sharing with you in this book, I told Mary I would work for him one day (another prophetic incident). This anointed teacher of the Word of God was Andrew

Wommack, a fellow Vietnam veteran, which God has called to minister His Word around the world, making disciples in every nation. Sure enough, three short years later, in 1983, we packed our belongings and children and headed off for Colorado Springs. I went to work for him for two years, in the communications department with light administrative duties. I basically did whatever I could do to help him, the ministry, and most of all, God, to get this glorious gospel of grace through Jesus Christ out to the world. During this time, God began bringing Vietnam veterans across my path, here and there, one at a time. Just seeing me, so many of them would start to cry, no matter how hard and tough they tried to appear to people around them. Their hearts would melt, become so tender, as we talked. The love of God began to really grow in my heart for them. Suddenly, I could understand their pain, their sorrow, their grief, and their anger and fear...but now I had some answers. I started sharing Philippians 3:13, 14 and John 3:16 with many of these veterans and received these responses: "I will never forget what happened in Vietnam." "I will never forget how I was treated when returning home." "I will never forgive or forget what the protesters did." "God could never forgive me for what I did in Vietnam." I have heard these statements and many others over the years. The statements pertaining to their forgiving and forgetting are very true in their own power. The statement about God not forgiving them is a lie of Satan. God has already forgiven us and is waiting for us to receive the forgiveness that He freely offers through His Son. Many have been raised religiously and believe that God stands with a large stick ready to swat you when out of line. Friend, this has never been farther from the truth! "For God so loved the world, that he gave his only begotten Son, that whosoever believeth in him should not perish, but have everlasting life. For God sent not his Son into the world to condemn the world; but that the world through him might be saved." (John 3:16, 17) The ability to forgive and then forget the offense can come only through the power of the Word of God (see notes on forgiveness). Comrades, isn't it time to let go of the past, lay it down and finish your life in peace and joy? Aren't you tired of making destructive choices, feeling guilty, having no genuine peace in your own heart, in your relationships, and no true joy in your life? "For the kingdom of God is not meat and drink; but righteousness, and peace, and joy in the Holy Ghost." (Romans 14:17) Before continuing, if you've never received Jesus Christ as the Lord and Savior of your life, I want to lead you in a simple prayer of salvation.

"Heavenly Father, I confess that I am a sinner. I thank you for sending your Son. I believe that Jesus Christ is the Messiah, was born of a virgin, died for my sin, and rose again. I confess Jesus as my Lord and Savior. I thank you, Father, for forgiving and saving me. In turn, I forgive all those whom I have resented, been bitter toward, or even hated. Amen."

God looks at the heart. If you have recognized your inability to help or save yourself, your need for Jesus Christ the Lord to save you, and if you prayed this prayer from your heart, you are saved. You have been born again. This is the first step in dealing with the past and healing. It is a new beginning. Your Christian journey is one of seeking the One who has loved you and saved you. It is knowing Him. It is one of finding out all He has done for you, who and what He has made you, and letting Him live His life through you, fulfilling all He has called you to (His purpose, will, and plan for your life). It is important that you find a good Word teaching church, read your Bible, pray (talk to God), listen for His voice to you, and receive the baptism of the Holy Spirit (see Bible study notes on Baptism in the Holy Spirit). "I indeed have baptized you with water: but he shall baptize you with the Holy Ghost." (Mark 1:8) Acts 19:2–6 tells us, "He said unto them, Have ye received the Holy Ghost since ye believed? And they said unto him, We have not so much as heard whether there be any Holy Ghost. And he said unto them, Unto what then were you baptized? And they said, Unto John's baptism. Then said Paul, John verily baptized with the baptism of repentance, saying unto the people, that they should believe on him which should come, that is, on Christ Jesus. When they heard this, they were baptized in the name of the Lord Jesus. And when Paul had laid his hands upon them, the Holy Ghost came on them; and they spake with tongues, and prophesied." You will need to be baptized in the Spirit to have a powerful prayer life, and to walk in the power of God. (Acts 1:8)

Even though I now had peace and the Vietnam issues were behind me, I had a greater desire to help other Vietnam veterans experience the life and love of God that I had received and was enjoying. I strongly felt God was leading me in a ministry to combat veterans, regardless of the war they fought in. I had left Andrew Wommack Ministries. Andrew and I are still good friends. I respect him as one of the greatest teachers of God's Word, in this generation.

I now turned back to the VA Vocational Rehab program once again. The counselor I saw gave me very good advice. He said, "Mike, an employer's first reaction comes from seeing your disability. You need a degree to prove to employers that the disability doesn't hold you back. It will show them that you can do the work." I took his advice and started back to school. I had a goal of obtaining a Bachelors Degree in Social Work (BSW) with a final goal of my Masters Degree in Social Work (MSW). Going to college was another new hurdle for me to conquer. I had been out of school for twenty years, wasn't confident that I could remember much of my high school studies, and I was blind and in a wheelchair on top of it. How would I see the blackboards? How would I take notes? How would I read the books? How would I take the tests? And how would I even get around the school by myself and find research material by myself? All these questions were flooding my mind. I was in turmoil. I attended my first three days at the University of Colorado at Colorado Springs, with severe apprehension. I found my greatest fears all very much a reality. I didn't know how I would do it. It was an impossible situation to me. I sought help from counselors and one instructor, but it seemed impossible to them, too. They said I would never do it. They encouraged me to quit, and find something else to do. I came home discouraged and depressed, and shared all this with Mary. I took their advice and quit. But Mary saw this as just another way the devil was trying to rob me. By this time, we both had enough knowledge of the Word to rise up, face this opposition and resist it with God's Word and prayer. In her loving and often persistent and persevering way, Mary told me, "That's a lie. You will make it. God will make a way. I don't know how, but I know he is the Way-Maker! You can do all things through Christ who strengthens you." We prayed together. My headache left. The nausea left. The peace of God came. I made phone calls to every place I could think of to find the way. God brought everything I needed and people to help me. I returned to school the next semester, using a tape recorder, magnifier, and every low vision aide available. This modern technology was great, but nothing like the team (Mary and I) working together again to overcome an obstacle. The most helpful thing was prayer and the Word. When it got hard I turned to God and His Word. He never failed me. He always showed me the way and brought me through. Mary was a continual support. She even did my typing until I received a computer with adaptive features, and at this point she gently said, "You are on your own." It was like a mother bird pushing her young out of the nest. The Holy Spirit helped me to become a very fast one-handed typist. He helped all the way through to victory. I graduated from New Mexico Highlands University, with honors and a Masters Degree in Social Work (MSW). God did abundantly above all I could ask or think. "Now unto him that is able to do exceeding abundantly above all that we ask or think, according to the power that worketh in us, Unto him be glory in the church by Christ Jesus throughout all ages, world without end. Amen" (Ephesians 3:20, 21).

I was hired by the Vet Center, where I had done my practicum, as a temporary, which later became a permanent position. I was a readjustment counselor, working with combat veterans that had been suffering from PTSD…the majority of them for years. I have no doubt that my time there was fruitful, and the veterans that really wanted to be free were helped and are well on their way to total recovery today. I left the Vet Center in 2001. After prayer and discussions with Mary, I made the decision to go back into retirement shortly after. I was so limited by government regulations as to how I could counsel the veterans. I am still counseling them on a smaller scale in my church and in my home. I am free to give them the Word of God that will make them free...not just give them coping skills I had learned from my college education and clinical experience. I am better equipped! "...If ye continue in my word, then are ye my disciples indeed; And ye shall know the truth, and the truth shall make you free." (John 8:31, 32) "If the Son therefore shall make you free, ye shall be free indeed." (John 8:36) The last few years have been dedicated to writing this book, again, with loving encouragement from Mary. I have also enjoyed spending more time with her, my children and their spouses, and now my five robust grandsons.

God has so completely delivered me from haunting Vietnam memories, and the negative emotions I was allowing to control my life from it all. Psalms 107:20 says "He sent His Word, and healed them, and delivered them from their destructions." Healing and deliverance are there for everyone, although the time frame may vary from person to person. It is an ongoing process and we must continually renew our mind with the scriptures. I once heard a brother say that your mind doesn't stay renewed any longer than your hair stays combed. I have not arrived myself, but I've left. I'm going forward. God is not a respecter of persons (Acts 10:34), "Then Peter opened his mouth and said, Of a truth I perceive that God is no respecter of persons:" What He has done for me, He will do for you.

Chapter Three: Developmental Years

In looking at the early developmental years of the Vietnam veteran, these views are based solely on my Midwest rural community upbringing, and my own speculations. The baby-boomers were raised by WWII fathers who returned home with the desire to get a good job, raise a family, and forget WWII. The father brought security, confidence, and discipline while mom brought nurturing and care giving. The returning WWII veteran had their issues, as well, and in many incidences became workaholics and turned to alcohol as a means of escape. The family didn't question why dad had an occasional binge with fellow veterans at the local veteran's club. The family structure was generally strong and good values and beliefs were taught. The "baby-boomers" in our rural farming community grew up with a strong work ethic, sense of trust, willingness to help others, knowledge of God and the Ten Commandments, etc. Our values and beliefs were not only learned at home, but were reinforced at school, at church, and in the community. The rural community churches provided summer Bible school, where the children could learn about God and have fun activities. We always looked forward to the fall, which brought the big community harvest party. The crops were in and now it was time to enjoy the company of neighbors. The kids enjoyed playing together and the grownups enjoyed fellowshipping with one another. The family not only worked together as a team, but enjoyed activities together (4-H Club, county/state fairs, carnivals, sports, etc). In most cases mothers were "stay-at-home" moms, who participated in local functions (church, school, community), but were always home when the children arrived home from school. Mom was always there to hear your stories and give encouragement. The family came together for dinner (supper) and enjoyed a home cooked meal around the table. The family then gathered around the television and watched shows such as *Father Knows Best, Leave It to Beaver, Laurence Welk, Ed Sullivan Show, Dinah Shore,* etc., which were all good family entertainment. Generally, the family stayed in one area, not like the transient society today.

The small rural farming community environment was very close knit and the Vietnam War brought families even closer together. As the young men were being drafted, the families banned together in support of each other. The young men were remembered in prayer and through the mailing of letters and packages. When the news of one being injured or killed came back home, the whole community grieved. It was this close-knit community that sent hundreds of cards and numerous packages to me while I was hospitalized.

The developmental years of today's soldiers (Persian Gulf War, Afghanistan and Iraqi wars) oftentimes are very different than those of most Vietnam veterans. Core Biblical beliefs are not taught or encouraged in many homes. Many families never darken the doors of a church. Biblical principles are taboo in our public schools, and the entertainment industry just reinforces all this "Godlessness." Divorce has taken its own toll in our society today. The young person often comes home to an empty house, either because both parents work or they are raised in a single parent home. In many cases, dad isn't around to help in the raising of the children, emotionally or financially. The single parent tries to fill both roles but it can't be done. The families are often uprooted because of job transfers, or just the urge for something different. Many children don't have mom there to hear about what happened at school that day. Being a "latchkey kid," is "the norm" for many. This leaves them unsupervised and often brings undesired behavior. The educational system has deteriorated with the removal of prayer and any mention of God, unless one attends a private school. Families become too busy and seldom enjoy the evening meal together. Instead of this being a time of communication and laughter, families grab bites "on the run," or the family eats their meals planted in front of the television set, watching their favorite shows while they eat. If their is a disagreement…no problem. Kids simply retreat to their own rooms to watch it on their own TV. Much of their time is spent playing video games, and strong work ethics have seemed to decline. Family communication is becoming a thing of the past. With abortion, sexual immorality, and the introduction of "euthanasia," young people are looking for the love, affection and attention they need and so desperately long for in all the wrong places. All of these social changes have had their affect on our young people, their values and their beliefs. However, even though the difference of the social environment changes from one generation to another, the "heart issue" of man has not changed since the fall of Adam. When he fell, the curse of death, in all of its manifestations and forms, came into the earth. Included in all this mess was fear, shame, guilt, pride, selfishness, depression, anxiety, discouragement, hopelessness, despair, resentment, bitterness, strife, hatred and murder, sorrow, grief, pain, weakness, distress, sickness and disease, greed, lack and poverty. Solomon said it this way in Ecclesiastes 1:9, 10, "The thing that hath been, it is that which shall be; and that which is done is that which shall be done: and there is no new thing under the sun. Is there anything whereof it may be said, See, this is new? It hath been already of old time, which was before us." Paul said it this way. "There hath no temptation taken you but such as is common to man…" (I Corinthians 10:13a) There is no new "muck and mire." But God did not leave us without hope. He had a plan from the foundation of the world to redeem mankind. He sent His Son, Jesus, to "buy back" what the devil had stolen from Adam, when Adam bowed his knee to Satan. The sacrifice of Jesus on the cross gave us back our righteous position before God, and right relationship with God, as His son or daughter, void of any shame, guilt or fear. He gave us back peace, love, joy, health and prosperity in every area of life. He gave us back the very life of God, eternal life, and the ability to know Him intimately. He gave us *Himself*, and all that He is! That's the good news of the Gospel!

At this time, it would be beneficial for you to write out the values and beliefs that were instilled in you during your first eighteen years of growing up. When you've completed this, mark them as positive or negative. Honesty is very important. Which of these values and beliefs changed during your military experience? Which ones did you completely "ditch" ("throw out the window")? Which ones did you hold on to, if any, and keep still today? Keep this paper close as we begin to explore how our military experience challenged every value and belief we ever thought we knew, hoped we knew, or believed we knew.

Let's look at the Vietnam War and what the military person was subjected to. The young men either enlisted (at times, an option rather than prison), or were drafted to serve their country. They left family, friends, and a comfortable, secure environment to be immediately thrust into a very rough and regimented one. The average age of the young men who served in the Vietnam War was nineteen. Some were as young as 17. The new soldier not only had to deal with being away from home, possibly for the first time, but they instantly met people of other cultural and ethnic backgrounds. We must remember this was during the long overdue Civil Rights movement and integration was immediate for the soldier. The soldier was exposed to racism. If there would have been some education on ethnicity and the different cultural backgrounds, many racial issues could have been avoided. Structure and training were needed to carry out military operations. The drill instructor (DI) became your new "mom," and believe me, they weren't as sweet, patient or as accommodating as her. The values and beliefs learned at home were about to be radically changed and not necessarily for the better.

The military became our second family. We looked to each other as brothers and became very close. The biggest challenged belief was "Thou shall not kill." During our training as infantrymen, we were trained to use various weapons (rifles, machine guns, grenades, mines, bayonets, etc.) and even taught hand-to-hand combat. It was during this training, that the drill instructors created a new mind set in each of us toward the Vietnamese people. The sergeants and lieutenants (who had already served previous tours), dehumanized them repeatedly to us. We eventually would develop our own attitude of superiority toward them because of their living conditions. This was all a part of the plan to make it easier to take another person's life. The American soldier soon realized that his enemy was very clever, and that your "junk" became their greatest weapon. Anything you threw away (even a can), they would take and make a "booby trap" out of it. The soldier was transported to Vietnam, saw an oppressed people, and often wondered why they were there. Once we were assigned to our units and went on our first mission, a new value was placed on life (our own, other American soldiers, and the Vietnamese people). Ours became more valuable. The life of the Vietnamese, less valuable. The survival instinct kicked in and every effort was made to return home after your tour. "Thou shall not kill" went "out the window."

It was war and we weren't sitting home watching a war flick on television anymore. We weren't playing video war games. This was the real deal! It was horrific! You never knew what was going to happen next. Your senses became very acute to every strange smell, sound, and even what you didn't hear. The GI did not like what he saw himself or his comrades turning into. Often the innocent were killed by accident or by retaliation. The war didn't have a bonafide front line, an age limit for the enemy, or the enemy marked by being in uniform, most of the time. The soldier was not only trying to survive, but would also receive continual reports on the protesting back home. It was bad enough trying to stay alive, without thinking about your own countrymen protesting the war. Many soldiers looked for a way of escape and turned to alcohol or drugs. These temporary ways of escape became an addictive pattern for so many returning Vietnam veterans. The Vietnam veteran, in many cases, left the combat zone and within forty-eight to seventy-two hours was back home. As he processed out of the service he was told not to discuss what he had seen or participated in, and to carry on as though nothing had happened. The returning soldier couldn't wait to catch his flight home to family and friends. He left the secure environment of the military base and was met by the war protestors, who welcomed him home by spitting on him, hurling things at him, and calling him "baby killer." The soldier had just returned from a war situation and reacted accordingly. He lashed out at the protestors and oftentimes found himself in jail, charged with assault and battery. He didn't expect this kind of homecoming. Those who never served have no idea what the Vietnam veteran faced and often times judged them harshly. Imagine yourself in this situation: (Your squad is patrolling through a village. A child leaves a group of adults and starts walking slowly toward you with their hands behind their back. As the child draws closer he/she suddenly hurls a grenade at you. Training and reaction take over. You seek cover and without a thought of age, you fire your weapon. It's you or him! You react and when the adrenaline rush is over you realize you killed a child. You are thankful that no American was killed or injured. The villagers gather around the child, comforting the crying parents, as you look at the dead child. Guilt and shame begin to invade your mind and heart, all related to the killing of a child. You start to withdraw, become sick to your stomach, fight back any emotions related to sorrow, and when able, you turn to alcohol or drugs to numb the pain.) Were you wrong for reacting as trained? If you were one of those quick to condemn, how would you have reacted?

This is just one example that the soldier serving in Vietnam faced. The young men who served in Vietnam were making life saving decisions, while those at home their age, were making decisions on what movie they should see, where they should eat, or where the party is this weekend, etc. The soldier grew up really fast, but not without its toll, and society couldn't understand the change. The returning soldiers often felt everyone was "out to get him." The veteran looked at everything as a life or death situation and often withdrew from society. Some returning veterans tried using their GI Bill but were met with great dissension by professors and students. The veteran was tired of fighting, didn't feel that anyone understood him, and withdrew even more. All the while more anger was building, and they couldn't express their feelings. The alcohol and drugs became a way of escape once more and often ended with jail time. Many veterans couldn't handle what society had to offer, so they went back to their "second family," who would understand them. Right here, at this point, many of them made the decision to make the military a career. With this decision usually came another tour in Vietnam. The soldier often volunteered to return to Vietnam for various reasons (revenge, respect of other soldiers, low self-esteem, etc). When their time came to leave Vietnam, they were relieved, but on the other hand, felt guilty for leaving friends behind. No doubt, our Iraqi war soldiers are facing some or all of these very same issues. A soldier is trained for war, but never totally prepared for what they will encounter.

Chapter Four: War's Memories

We looked at some obstacles facing young soldiers. Yes, these were drastic changes at a critical developmental age. The young soldier faced death on a daily basis. He was forced to make split-second decisions (life or death; sometimes right, sometimes wrong), kill mankind (young and old), hold a wounded friend (often with them dying in your arms), a rotating replacement military, and then returning to their homelands as the bad guy. This last issue, thank God, pertains only to the Vietnam veteran. (We have learned from our mistakes.) The young soldier had neither time to express emotions on the battlefield, nor any closure (grief) over those friends killed, wounded, or rotating out. The veteran continually stuffed his emotions, and/or turned to substance abuse to numb the pain. Returning soldiers had already participated in war, but when returning home, realized they couldn't legally drink or vote, and it made them even angrier that they could risk their life, but not enjoy certain freedoms at home. The Vietnam veteran, like the WWII veteran, was ready to seek employment, start a family, and put the war experience behind. Many married and started a family, but still had unresolved issues from their military time plaguing them, which led to divorce, and in many situations, domestic violence preceding it. A resentment started mounting toward those that never served and who, seemingly, had a head start (better jobs, homes, marriages, etc). For many of them, after they had babies with birth defects, babies that died in their first year of life, and experienced disabling symptoms in their own bodies, found out they had been exposed to Agent Orange (a chemical our government used to destroy foliage in the jungles). Persian Gulf veterans faced exposure to burning oil and chemical gases from the enemy that left them with respiratory problems, loss of memory, muscular/skeletal problems and more.

Add this brick to the load, and now we have shame, guilt, anger, resentment, envy, blame, sorrow, grief, fear, and the list grows. I once heard a Bible teacher use the acronym "garbage" which stood for guilt, anger, resentment, blame, anxiety, grief, and envy. He wasn't referring to a combat veteran, but the acronym fits very well. Is it a wonder that so many of our veterans deal with psychological problems? The Wall has the names of 58,000 men and women who died in Vietnam. It doesn't include those still listed as MIA's or those who have committed suicide because of the mental torment. The veteran sometimes seeks help in many ways (drugs, alcohol, VA programs, private programs, and withdrawal from society). These are all temporary fixes. How many times, and for how many years, can you attend sessions on anger management, stress reduction, self-esteem classes, etc. and never get anywhere...never move forward...never overcome...never get truly free? We are dealing with a spiritual issue and it can be healed only by a relationship and fellowship with God, by His Spirit and through His Word. He's the One who created you, knows what broke you, and knows how to fix you!

Psychiatrists, psychologists, clinical therapists, etc. seem quick to label a person with a psychological disorder. The veteran receives the label, placed on medication to cover symptoms, termed unemployable, and immediately justifies his actions because of the label. The person has now become the diagnosis rather than a person with a disability. It is easier to blame everything on the diagnosis (PTSD) rather than take responsibility for his actions. The sad thing is that those around him suffer, and in many instances he controls the family with, what I call, "the PTSD excuse." An example: A veteran comes home from a stressful day at work wanting a relaxing evening at home. His wife greets him with "I didn't have time to cook dinner this evening." Immediately, without waiting for an explanation, he snaps back sharply, and an argument follows. The veteran either retreats to another room, or heads for the nearest bar where he can unwind. He returns home late and expects his wife to be romantic, but finds a cold shoulder. This generates anger again, and what should have been resolved hours earlier, escalates. The next thing he knows is that the police have arrived and he is charged with domestic violence and has a restraining order placed on him. This veteran, having been diagnosed with PTSD, immediately blames the disability for his actions. This was, and still may be, a very common scenario in the lives of the veteran suffering from PTSD. In all the years of my counseling these veterans, this was a pretty standard answer to any question concerning their negative behavior. Sadly enough, most of them really believe they can't help it. They believe their behavior is out of their control. They've been schooled and trained to believe it's true. However, I propose to you, that even at the height of his worst moment, this same veteran still has a will to choose life, instead of death, blessing instead of cursing, peace instead of strife, love instead of anger and malice. His negative behavior can be stopped. The veteran can learn to master his emotions, instead of letting them control or master him, by changing the way he thinks. Deuteronomy 30:19 says, "I call heaven and earth to record this day against you, that I have set before you life and death, blessing and cursing: therefore *choose* life, that both thou and thy seed may live." The reader may now be saying to himself, "Wait a minute. Stress, anger, relationship problems, alcohol, and withdrawal are all symptoms of my PTSD." This is a fact, but we are going to deal with *truth*. Jesus said, "Thy Word is truth." (John 17:17) And John 14:6a declares (Jesus, Himself, speaking), "Jesus saith unto him, I am the way, the truth, and the life." What about the person who reacted in the same manner and received the same consequences, but doesn't have PTSD? It is time to look at it as it really is! You have to make the decision to change and it can't be done by yourself! Psalms 107:20 says "He sent His word and healed them, and delivered them from their destructions."

The good news is that you don't have to carry these burdens any longer. It is time to lay those burdens at the foot of the cross and leave them there. Do not pick them back up. "Come to Me, all you who labor and are heavy laden, and I will give you rest. Take My yoke upon you and learn from Me, for I am gentle and lowly in heart, and you will find rest for your soul. For My yoke is easy and My burden is light." Matt. 11:28–30. The person who has received Jesus Christ as his Lord and Savior has been freed from bondage. "For as much then as the children are partakers of flesh and blood, he also himself likewise took part of the same; that through death he might destroy him that had the power of death, that is, the devil; And deliver them who through fear of death were all their lifetime subject to bondage." (Hebrews 2:14, 15) John 8:36 says, "If the Son therefore shall make you free, ye shall be free indeed." When you received Jesus you became a brand new creation. "Therefore, if anyone is in Christ, he is a new creation; old things have passed away; behold, old things have became new" (II Corinthians 5:17) When you received the Lord, you were instantly changed. You now have the spirit of Christ and have been forgiven of *all* sin…past, present, future. This means *every* wrong thing you have done intentionally, or unintentionally, during the war, now, and how you will fall short and miss the mark tomorrow. You have been given a new nature, God's very own nature! Your spirit has been changed. It has been reborn. It looks like God. It thinks like God. It talks like God. It obeys God. It pleases God. It does not sin! However, you also have a soul, which is your mind, will and emotions, and you live in a body. Paul often referred to this mortal body as your "tent." I have heard it called your "earth suit." It's what you need to be "legal" on this earth. Even though your spirit is in this wonderfully regenerated state, your soul and body are not. Your mind must be renewed every day, by meditating on God's Word. Psalm 1:1–3 shows us that a life spent meditating on God's Word, daily, bears much fruit, and prospers in every way (spiritually, mentally, emotionally, physically, socially, and financially). "Blessed is the man that walketh not in the counsel of the ungodly, nor standeth in the way of sinners, nor sitteth in the seat of the scornful. But his delight is in the law of the *Lord*; and in his law doeth he meditate day and night. And he shall be like a tree planted by the rivers of water, that bringeth forth his fruit in his season; his leaf also shall not wither; and whatsoever he doeth shall prosper." Even though meditation mainly involves pondering, thinking and considering, meditation certainly includes speaking His Word out of your mouth, repeatedly…more accurately, muttering over and over. Meditation brings revelation. And when revelation drops in your heart, transformation takes place. Romans 12:1, 2 tells us, "I beseech you therefore, brethren, by the mercies of God, that ye present your bodies a living sacrifice, holy, acceptable unto God, which is your reasonable service. And be not conformed to this world: but be ye transformed by the renewing of your mind, that ye may prove what is that good, and acceptable, and perfect will of God."

I have discovered that the beginning of healing and deliverance from war trauma, or PTSD resulting from war, is in a decision to do two things: First, to realize one's need for a relationship with God by receiving or accepting His forgiveness which He extends through His Son, Jesus Christ. I covered this in Chapter II. And second, to forgive all those who have wronged you, including, and especially, those who have wronged you during your military service and combat. This has to include forgiving the very enemy you were in combat against, government officials, and even war protestors that you felt were not supportive of your position and job as a soldier. Once you realize that God has, once and for all, forgiven you of *all* sin, and received (welcomed and accepted) that forgiveness, you are free to forgive others the same way God has forgiven you.

Chapter Five: Forgiven

As for the veteran who thinks he can never be forgiven, let's look at some Biblical examples. First, let's look at King David (II Samuel, chapter 11). It was a time for kings to be at war but David stayed back. While walking about on the roof of his house, David noticed Bathsheba bathing, and sent for her. He committed adultery with his loyal servant's wife. This wasn't enough. He sent for Uriah, intending to bring Uriah and Bathsheba together intimately, to relieve his own guilt, and, I believe, so David would not be found out, if conception took place. (There was no DNA testing in those days!) The Bible says, "She was purified from her uncleanness." They both had to know there was a possibility that she could conceive. But, as long as both David and Bathsheba kept quiet, people would think the child was Uriah's. This plan didn't work because of Uriah's loyalty to David, and believing this pleasure was not right while his comrades were out to war. David summoned Uriah after he found out that he hadn't gone home. David gave him a written message to hand deliver to his commander. Uriah didn't know that he was carrying his own death sentence. He was placed on the front lines and killed by the enemy as his troops pulled back from him. King David not only committed adultery, but also had Uriah murdered. I don't believe that David originally wanted or sought to kill Uriah. This is where his lying (deceit and guile) took him. I had a pastor once who repeatedly told us from the pulpit, "Sin will take you farther than you want to go, keep you longer than you want to stay, and cost you more than you want to pay." Look at I Samuel 13:14 and Acts 13:22, where David is called a man after God's own heart. It was, obviously, not because of his sin, but rather, because of his contrite and penitent heart. He was totally forgiven by God. We know this because II Samuel 12:13 says, "And David said unto Nathan, I have sinned against the *Lord*.

And Nathan said unto David, The *Lord* also hath put away thy sin; thou shalt not die." David, himself, said, in Psalm 103:1–3, "Bless the *Lord*, O my soul: and all that is within me, bless his holy name. Bless the *Lord*, O my soul, and forget not all his benefits: Who forgiveth all thine iniquities..."

The second person we will look at is Simon Peter. Here is an apostle that walked with Jesus, saw the miracles, heard the teachings, but still denied knowing Jesus. Matthew 16:16, 17 gives the account of Peter's revelation that Jesus was the Son of God. "And Simon Peter answered and said, Thou art the Christ, the Son of the living God. And Jesus answered and said to him, "Blessed art thou, Simon Barjona: for flesh and blood hath not revealed it unto thee, but my Father, which is in heaven." Even though Peter was given this revelation he still questioned Jesus. Let's look at Luke 5:5–8 where Peter questioned Jesus' knowledge of fishing, "And Simon answering said unto him, Master, we have toiled all the night, and have taken nothing: nevertheless at thy word I will let down the net. And when they had this done, they enclosed a great multitude of fishes: and their net brake. And they beckoned unto their partners, which were in the other ship, that they should come and help them. And they came, and filled both the ships, so that they began to sink. When Simon Peter saw it, he fell down at Jesus' knees, saying, Depart from me; for I am a sinful man, O Lord." Jesus didn't leave Peter, but rather kept him at His side. When Jesus and the disciples were at the Mount of Olives prior to His betrayal, Jesus gave Peter some shocking news. "Jesus said unto him, Verily I say unto thee, That this night, before the cock crow, thou shalt deny me thrice." (Matt. 26:34). Peter didn't believe this would ever happen, but as we see in the following account, it was just as Jesus said. "Then saith the damsel that kept the door unto Peter, Art not thou also one of this man's disciples? He saith, I am not." "And Simon Peter stood and warmed himself. They said therefore unto him, Art not thou also one of his disciples? He denied it, and said, I am not. One of the servants of the high priest, being his kinsman whose ear Peter cut off, saith, Did not I see thee in the garden with him? Peter then denied again:

and immediately the cock crew" (John 18:17, 25–27). Jesus is Love, full of mercy and compassion. Mark 16:6–7 tells us that the angel sent by the Lord singled out Peter, mentioning Him by name, when he said to the women who went to the tomb, after He had risen, "And he saith unto them, Be not affrighted: Ye seek Jesus of Nazareth, which was crucified: he is risen; he is not here: behold the place where they laid him. But go your way, tell his disciples *and Peter* that he goeth before you into Galilee: there shall ye see him, as he said unto you." God's angels do not say anything God does not tell them to say. "Bless the *Lord*, ye his angels, that excel in strength, that do his commandments, hearkening unto the voice of His Word" (Psalms 103:20). I really believe that God instructed that angel at the tomb to specifically include Peter, to let him and all the disciples know that He had forgiven him (Peter) and them. Jesus was letting Peter and all of them know that his love for Peter and the rest had not changed. They had *all* forsaken him at one point. "But all this was done, that the scriptures of the prophets might be fulfilled. Then *all* the disciples forsook him, and fled." (Matthew 26:56) Oh, my friend, this same Love, mercy and forgiveness is available and being extended to you today. "Jesus Christ, the same yesterday, and to day and for ever." (Hebrews 13:8) "For God so loved the world, that he gave his only begotten Son, that *whosoever* believeth in him, should not perish, but have everlasting life." Jesus said in John 6:37b, "and him that cometh to me I will in no wise cast out."

The third person is Saul of Tarsus (Paul). In Acts 7:58 we see Saul witnessing the stoning of Stephen. Then as we move to chapter 8, Saul is requesting permission to bring Christians before the Jewish rulers. He took part in persecuting Christians. As we continue we see Saul's encounter with the Lord on the Damascus Road. Saul had two questions "Who are you Lord?" and "What shall I do?" (Acts 9:1–22). He was instantly transformed and started serving the Lord. Paul wrote two-thirds of the New Testament giving his revelation to the body of Christ. He calls himself the "chief of sinners" in I Timothy 1:15. Look at this in the light of being a combat veteran, and the shame or guilt the veteran has carried all these years. Don't you think that Paul was reminded of his past actions by the devil? Of course he was! The difference is that Paul had the revelation of God's love and forgiveness offered to and extended toward him. Yes, it is possible to be free from shame and guilt. It is our decision to welcome, receive and accept God's love and forgiveness offered to and extended toward us. His forgiveness is freely given. There is nothing you have done that Jesus' blood has not already paid for. You are forgiven! Just believe and receive that for yourself! How sad it would be for you to remain in "your prison cell," with the prison doors open, and your acquittal paid for in full. It is obvious in these three instances how merciful God is, and these are only three examples. The Word of God is full of examples and revelation of God's loving-kindness and mercy. Malachi 3:6a says, "For I am the *Lord*, I do not change;" The Word also says that God is no respecter of persons (Acts 10:34). If God forgave the world (every man) of their sin, on that cross, no matter what you might have done, He forgave you. And He did! The problem, then, you see, isn't with God forgiving man, but rather men refusing to accept His love and forgiveness, thereby rejecting Him and His plan to save them (salvation). My friend, do not go one more day, one more hour, not even any farther than this page in this book without receiving for yourself, God's love and forgiveness through Jesus Christ, His plan of salvation. Once you've done this, it is imperative that you forgive yourself, as David, Peter, Paul and a multitude of others have done. You will not go forward without forgiving yourself. It's a choice to believe and receive God's forgiveness toward you. And it's a choice to forgive yourself. It is done by faith, not a feeling. To say you can't forgive yourself is to esteem yourself higher than God, because God has already forgiven you. You are not greater than Him! (II Chronicles 2:7). If God forgave you, you can forgive you!

Second, you must forgive all those who have offended you, wronged, hurt you and treated you unjustly. This can actually be easy, if you meditate on one thing...all the rotten things God has forgiven you of. Just think about all the times you offended people, you wronged people, you hurt people, and treated them unjustly…and all the rejection and mockery you voiced toward the Lord, before you came to Him. If you'll read Isaiah, chapter 53, and meditate on it, you'll get a glimpse of the price Jesus paid for your forgiveness, how He let you "off the hook" and you won't have any trouble letting someone else "off the hook." That's exactly what forgiveness from the heart is. It is letting the offender go free, the same way Jesus let you go free for the debt you owed Him. Jesus paid your debt for you. In the 18th chapter of Matthew, Peter asked Jesus just how many times he had to forgive someone of the same thing. Jesus told him "seventy times seven" *in one day!* He went on to tell the disciples a parable about a man who owed a great debt to his lord. The master was going to make him pay with everything he had, including his wife and children, but when the servant fell down and worshiped him and pleaded for mercy, his lord forgave him the debt and let him go. Shortly after, this same servant went out and one of his fellow servants owed him a small debt. This servant would not forgive the man his debt, though he pled for mercy. The servant had him thrown in prison. "Then his lord, after that he had called him, said unto him, O thou wicked servant, I forgave thee all that debt, because thou desiredst me: Shouldest not thou also have had compassion on thy fellow servant, even as I had pity on thee?" (Matthew 18:32, 33) Friend, pray this prayer from your heart, by faith, not by anything you are feeling in your emotions, but out of obedience to God and His Word. God will honor your heart in wanting to do the right thing, and the forgiveness process will begin. Forgive all those who have wronged you, especially your enemy in war, government officials, and war protestors. Put their names in the blanks everywhere except where it says to name the offense. "Lord, I confess I've had unforgiveness, bitterness and resentment toward _____. I confess it as sin. I thank you for forgiving me, Lord. The same way you have forgiven me, I choose to forgive _____ from my heart. _____ owes me nothing. Jesus paid _____ debt to me. I acquit _____. I free _____. I clear _____ from the charge of _____ (name the offense). I let _____ off. I release _____. I discharge _____ from any duty to me. I deem

_____ "not guilty" of _____ (name the offense), because Jesus does. I pardon _____. I pass over _____ offense toward me like they never did it. I free _____ from the consequences of _____ (name the offense). I grant _____ pardon without harboring resentment. I do not demand punishment. I do not demand that _____ "set it right," remedy or rectify the situation, or "pay me back." I do not demand that _____ make amends for what they did. I overlook _____ sin. I give all resentment, indignation, ill will or malice (wanting something bad to happen to _____) as a result of their sin. I give up all anger aroused by this unjust and mean act. I let it drop. I never mention it again—to _____ or anyone else. I cease (stop) consideration of the matter. I refuse to think about it anymore. I relieve _____ from any debt or obligation to me. I let it go. I liberate _____, and in so doing I am liberated. It's over. I bless _____. I forget it.

You are probably saying about now, "Now wait a minute. I can forgive them, but I cannot forget it. This is not true, my friend. It is a choice just like believing, receiving, and forgiving. It is a decision we must make. God says in Jeremiah 31:34 that He will remember our sin no more. Now, if anybody could remember everything it would be God. It's a choice He has made. He has chosen to forget our sin. We can too! Philippians 3:13,14 says (Paul speaking), "Brethren, I count not myself to have apprehended: but this one thing I do, forgetting those things which are behind, and reaching forth unto those things which are before, I press toward the mark for the prize of the high calling of God in Christ Jesus." This is the same man that referred to himself as the "chief of sinners" to Timothy, and in II Corinthians 7:2 said he had wronged no man. Now I would say that's a man that chose to forget some things. Your mind, friend, is like a computer. It has those "hidden files" which will come up only on command. You might be saying, "I don't command my memories of war to come to me." Don't you? What do you spend your time meditating on? Certain things you hear, see, taste, smell or feel can bring a war memory to you, but it's what you do with that thought that counts, friend. Generally, many Vietnam veterans listen to the "oldies" music station of the '60's, watch every Vietnam war flick, and continually reminisce their "war stories" with other veterans, through conversation and old photographs. They think and talk about it all the time. They sit in "therapy groups," week after week, year after year, hashing the same "stuff" over and over and over again. They've been "brainwashed" that they have a chronic disease, and will never get well, and until they hear the truth, most of them believe that and receive that lie. They keep going to "therapy" to learn how to "cope," but nothing ever changes. And this veteran wonders why he is still having nightmares and pent up anger in his life. For some of them, there is a "pay off," to staying sick, and they don't really want to get well. For others, they want to get well, but just don't know how. They've never heard the *truth*. I, personally, quit watching Vietnam War movies shortly after coming home from the war. I was very aware, even then, before knowing the Lord, what they did to me. Only on occasion, do I hash over an old war story (except to minister). Reminders of the Vietnam War are there for me every day that I get out of bed, without eyesight, without legs and with only one well functioning hand. Yes, I am reminded of Vietnam on a daily basis, and could think on that all day long, if I wanted to, if I chose to. However, the life of Paul has taught me many things. I have received God's love and forgiveness for me, forgave those who had wronged me, and, yes, had to choose every day of my life to forget it, in the beginning. I just don't go there. If thoughts of shame, guilt, fear, failure, discouragement, hopelessness, feeling sorry for myself, etc. come, I cast them down, and think on something better…God, His Word, all He's done for me and who I am in Him! And, truthfully, now, negative thoughts about the war in Vietnam and its toll on my soul and body don't even enter my mind. If I wanted to, I could dredge them up all over again, and go back to that life of hell and bondage, just by taking my eyes off of God and His Word, by going back to that negative thought life I lived in for so many years, but what in the world for?!? It's not glorifying to God. It's not pleasing to Him. It's not uplifting. It's not life giving. It's not abundant life! It's certainly not "the mind of Christ." It's death, in all of its

MICHAEL E. PETERSEN, MSW

manifestations and forms. Who needs it? And who wants it? And this brings me to the last three chapters of this book...how to master all the negative emotions and change the negative behavior that is associated with and so prevalent among our soldiers and veterans returning from war, those clinically diagnosed with PTSD, and those that have not been diagnosed, but know they just haven't "been themselves" since they returned home from war. You can be free if you want to be! Read on!

Chapter Six:
Overcoming with the Word

The DSM-IV, produced by the American Psychiatric Association for the mental health professional, contains the diagnosis and criteria for PTSD. The publication of the diagnosis and criteria will not be included because of copyright restrictions and the tendency for people to try to "self diagnose." The mental health professional would use individual and group therapy using cognitive/behavioral models. The therapist, by educating the client on anger management, stress management, dealing with grief, and building your self-esteem, attempts to change the thinking process and how you react to a given situation. I will address these areas based on a Biblical deliverance through the scriptures. I can't stress enough the importance of renewing your mind with the Word of God. Sitting in therapy and group sessions takes time out of your day, and so will prayer and the Word. But you never "sow to the Spirit," and reap corruption, only life everlasting. "...but he that soweth to the Spirit shall of the Spirit reap life everlasting." (Galatians 6:8) The rewards you reap from prayer and time spent meditating in God's Word will produce life eternal, inside you. God changes you from the inside out. It is not you trying in your own strength to change yourself on the outside. It is the best investment you will ever make for your spirit, soul and body, and in all reality, for the good of others. The witness of your life and time spent with God will make them hungry and thirsty for Him, and you will be strengthened to be able to help to them. God says you will, literally, be *transformed* by the power of God, as you begin to "think like God thinks." "For I am not ashamed of the gospel (the good news) of Christ: for it is the *power* of God unto salvation to every one that believeth..." (Romans 1:16) and

Romans 12:2 says that we are "transformed by the renewing of our mind." Isaiah tells us that God's thoughts are higher than our thoughts, and His ways higher than our ways, but God never said we couldn't know them. As a matter of fact in I Corinthians 2:9 and10, Paul writes "But as it is written, Eye hath not seen, nor ear heard, neither have entered into the heart of man, the things which God hath prepared for them that love him, But God hath revealed them unto us by his Spirit: for the Spirit searcheth all things, yea, the deep things of God." And one of the greatest revelations you'll ever walk in, is "Blessed is the man that walketh not in the counsel of the ungodly, nor standeth in the way of sinners, nor sitteth in the seat of the scornful. *But his delight is in the law of the Lord; and in His law doeth he meditate day and night.* And he shall be like a tree planted by the rivers of water, that bringeth forth his fruit in his season; his leaf also shall not wither; and whatsoever he doeth shall prosper." God told Joshua, before taking Jericho, "This book of the law shall not depart out of thy mouth; but thou shalt *meditate therein day and night*, that thou mayest observe to *do* according to all that is written therein: for *then* thou shalt make thy way prospereth, and then thou shalt have good success." (Joshua 1:8) Meditation of God's Word will bring revelation that drops in your heart and there it is conceived. The Word is a seed. Peter refers to it as the "incorruptible seed." (I Peter 1:23) It has the power in itself to reproduce after its kind. (Genesis 1:11, 12) And it will do just that, if you apply it to any area of your life that needs change or transformation.

Trauma—We can't deny the event having happened in our life, whether it is war related, rape, abuse, natural disaster, or whatever. What we can and must do is to take the whole mess to the cross, to Jesus, where it was all paid for by His blood. Give it to Him! "Casting all your care him; for he careth for you." (I Peter 5:7) If He is caring for you, you don't have to bear that burden. You put the burden of it on Him. His yoke is easy and His burden is light. (Matthew 11:30) Then, begin to take responsibility for your emotions. I cannot say this enough. *You can master your emotions!!!* It's a lie of Satan to think otherwise. You may have been a victim but you never have to remain a victim. You can come out of a victim mentality. Renew your mind to *these* simple, but, oh so powerful, truths. If you have been born again by the Spirit of God, you have now become the victor, not a victim. II Corinthians 2:14 says, "Now thanks be unto God, which *always* causeth us to *triumph* in *Christ...*" Romans 8:37 tells us, "Nay, in *all* these things we are more than *conquerors* through *Him* that loved us." And Paul had just listed a whole mess of horrible situations under which men find themselves at times...tribulation, distress, persecution, famine, nakedness, peril or sword. I John 4:4 says, "Ye are of God, little children, and have *overcome* them: because *greater* is He who is in you than he who is in the world." I John 5:4 makes our victory clear. "For whatsoever (are you a whatsoever?) is born of God overcometh the world: and this is the victory that overcometh the world, even our faith." Yes, the event happened. Take it to Jesus, deal with the forgiveness issues we discussed earlier, choose to forget it and move on with your life. When the memories come, don't meditate on them. Cast those thoughts down. "Casting down imaginations, and every high thing that exalteth itself against the knowledge of God, and bringing into captivity *every thought* to the obedience of Christ." (II Corinthians 10:5) Make a deliberate choice to think on other things. You don't have to think on any old thought that enters your mind. I once thought I couldn't help what I thought on. But when I found out that I could, it changed my life. I heard a preacher once say, "I can't stop a bird from flying over my head, but I can stop it from building a nest in my hair." "Finally, brethren, whatsoever things are true, whatsoever things are honest, whatsoever things are just, whatsoever things are pure, whatsoever things are lovely, whatsoever things are of good report, if there be any virtue, and if there be any praise, think on these things." (Phil. 4:8). Be patient! It is through faith and patience that we inherit the promises of God. (Hebrews 6:12 and Hebrews 10:36.) It is a process. Unlike Superman, you will not change overnight. Your spirit was changed in an instant, when you received the Lord, but it takes time to "reprogram" this old brain of ours. But don't get discouraged, and by all means, don't give up...because...if you *continue* in God's Word, you will be His disciple, indeed, and you will know the Truth and the Truth will make you free. Just keep loving Jesus, live a life devoted to Him and His Word, get involved in and stay in a healthy, life-giving church (assembly or body of believers), and you can not do anything but change and grow more and more into His image. The person who chooses to meditate on negative circumstances or problems, instead of the solution (God's Word), will find themselves an emotional wreck and looking for an escape (alcohol, sex, drugs, etc). The answer to a spiritual problem is not alcohol, not drugs, not a perverted sexual lifestyle, not "shopping 'til you drop." It is in giving your life to Christ, developing an intimate prayer life with Him, (staying connected with His presence all day long), and keeping your mind renewed with God's Word.

Feelings—When trauma occurs, the person feels tremendous fear, horror, and/or helplessness, all a result of the unknown. The person has no knowledge of how or why it happened. The fear that comes with such severe trauma is so magnified at that time, it buries itself deep in the soul (heart) of that person and returns over and over again, especially when triggered by some sort of stimuli related to the incident (i.e. thoughts, words, dreams, music, the same place, the same incident, etc.) And if this fear is not addressed and dealt with by the blood of Jesus, the Spirit of God and His Word, the person can take it to their grave. This fear produces the symptoms of PTSD we discussed earlier (depression, anxiety, sleeplessness, withdrawal/ isolation, nightmares, flashbacks, anger outbursts, startle response, relationship issues, substance abuse, survivor's guilt, etc.). Brothers and sisters, we must not allow fear to control our lives! Fear connects you to demonic forces and the death they generate. *It is not of God*, in any way, shape or form! "For God hath not given us the spirit of fear; but of power, and of love, and of a sound mind." II Timothy 1:7. Romans 8:15 says, "For ye have *not* received the spirit of bondage again to fear; but ye have receive the Spirit of adoption, whereby we cry, Abba, Father." And, Isaiah writes in chapter 54, verse 11, "O thou afflicted, tossed with tempest, and not comforted..." He continues in verse 14, with His promise of freedom to this afflicted and tormented one, "In righteousness shalt thou be established: thou shalt be far from oppression; for thou shalt not fear: and from terror; for it shall not come near thee." Fear has torment. (I John 4:18) Anybody ever bound by such fear knows the torment that John talks about here. It is "hell on earth," and it is what puts people every day into mental hospitals and the grave. The person who allows fear to rule their life will always be controlled by it. It will tell them exactly what they can and can't do. These people develop depression, anxiety, panic attacks (and these are very real, by the way), etc., and never want to leave their home. Their home usually becomes the only "safe" place (in their mind), where they feel "halfway" in control, though they are not. Oftentimes, they become totally dependent on others. This fear begins to affect every area of their lives, slowly, but surely. It not only rules their life, but they control others with their fear. Control is always born out of fear. These oppressed ones begin to fear leaving the house and at the same time they are afraid to be alone. This, my friend, is the epitome of bondage. Medication is often given for depression, anxiety, mood swings, anger, etc, but it never gets to the root of the problem. It is only a "cover-up." It only masks symptoms of a greater problem, a spiritual problem. The side effects from these medications are uncomfortable, and at the very least, can be horrific or long term. Pharmaceutical drugs were never designed for long-term usage, but rather a short-term while issues are being addressed, but doctors are prescribing these anti-depressant/anxiety drugs for people for life. They have no problem with their patients living on these year after year. And the funny thing is, even after years on these drugs, most are still experiencing all the symptoms of depression, anxiety, and panic attacks. I counseled hundreds of veterans and have seen my share of countless people, in general, with this same scenario. *This is not life!* This is no way to live. I'm not saying that some medication isn't necessary, in some cases, however, even so, why not believe God for a better life while you're taking it? Why not believe to be freed from PTSD, and from taking prescription drugs the rest of your life? There is a better life! You can be free from all that oppression. You can be free from taking "mood-altering" drugs that, frankly, usually leave you cloudy and foggy most of the time, and distressed from their numerous other side effects. God wants you free! This is why Jesus came…to destroy the works of the devil! (I John 3:8) It is His will, His desire, His plan and promise to liberate you from this prison. This can't be emphasized enough! Remember what Jesus said in Luke 4:18, 19, "The Spirit of the *Lord* is upon me, because He hath anointed me to preach the gospel to the poor; He hath sent me to heal the brokenhearted, to preach deliverance to the captives and recovering of sight to the blind, to set at liberty them that are bruised, to preach the acceptable year of the *Lord*." And Jesus told us in John 4:24, that whoever the Son sets free, is free indeed. God has medicine, too, for every spiritual, mental, emotional and physical ailment, disorder, syndrome, or disease. *It is His Word!!* Proverbs 4:20 tells us, "My son, *attend* to *My words; incline thine ear* unto *My sayings. Let them not depart from thine eyes; keep them in the midst of thine heart. For they are life unto those that find them, and health to all their flesh.*" If you look up that word, "health," in your concordance, you will find the Hebrew meaning to be, "medicine." Your deliverance from fear will come from the revelation of these five scriptures—Hebrews 2:14, 15 ("Forasmuch then as the children are partakers of flesh and blood, he (Jesus) also himself likewise took part of the same that through death he might destroy him that had the power of death, that is, the devil; and deliver them who through fear of death were all their lifetime subject to bondage.") John 17:23 ("I in them, and thou in me, that they may be made perfect in one; and that the world may know that thou has sent me, and *hast loved them, as thou hast loved Me.*") Isaiah 41:10 ("Fear thou not; *for I am with thee*: be not dismayed; for I am thy God: *I will strengthen thee*; yea, *I will help thee*; yea, *I will uphold thee* with the right hand of my righteousness.") Hebrews 13:5 ("…for he hath said, I will never leave thee, nor forsake thee.") And II Corinthians 5:21 ("For he hath made him (Jesus) to be sin for us, who knew no sin; that we might be made the righteousness of God in him." If you will begin to meditate on these five scriptures, brothers and sisters, you will receive the *revelation* (not head knowledge, or mental assent), but heart knowledge of these five truths: God loves you as much as He loves Jesus, that He is with you and will never leave or forsake you, that Jesus has already delivered you from the fear of death (in all of its manifestations and forms), and that you are the righteousness of God in Christ. You have been made righteous (freely justified, not guilty and in right standing with God) by grace through faith. If you get heart revelation of these truths, friend, fear cannot stay. It will leave. I John 4:15–19 tells us that perfect love casts out fear! A revelation of God's love for you and walking in that love toward others will drive fear right out of your life. And James tells us, chapter 4, verse 7, "Submit yourselves therefore to God. Resist the devil, and he will flee from you." Think on *these things*!

I will discuss some of the most frequently seen symptoms associated with PTSD, and as you read these symptoms, let's look at those that are under your control. Reading on in this chapter may anger you some, because you may feel and even really believe like they are out of your control. You may be saying, even at this moment, "You don't understand. You don't know what you're talking about. I can't help it. I can't control myself." I know that may be what you feel and believe, but that's what we're here to change…what you believe! Feelings, which have nothing to do with faith, will come later, as you set your heart in the right direction to believe God's Word, the Way, the Truth, the Life, (John 14:6) over what you feel. The truth is, that you can control your negative emotions with the power of the Holy Spirit and His Word, (your sword…Ephesians 6:17). The belief that you can't is the lie you need to reject, refuse, renounce and resist.

As you continue to read on, friends, ask the Lord to uncover every hidden negative motive or thing in your heart, concerning all this, and you will get free. I believe, even now, as you are hearing His Word, faith is coming, and God is flooding your heart with Light. I believe He is opening the eyes of your understanding. Ask Him for wisdom. He is faithful. He will answer all your questions and there is nothing He can't or won't make clear to you. God will give you all the grace, help and strength you need to make honest confessions to

Him, and repent of anything He shows you that is ungodly and not glorifying to Him. He corrects us for our benefit. (Hebrews 12:5–13) He knows the way to *life*, and He wants you to experience it more than you do. As you do all this, you will certainly find that you are more in control than you thought. After all, self-control is a "fruit of the Spirit" (Galatians 5:22).

It is a difficult thing to accept the fact that you may be using these symptoms and negative behavior patterns to control others. And it is a hard thing to admit that they "come in handy," when you need them to excuse your behavior. It is also easier to blame the diagnosis for your actions than to take responsibility, a word that most veterans, and people, in general, don't want to hear. It reminds me of the old Flip Wilson saying, "The devil made me do it." No, you made the conscious decision to react the way you reacted. Now, that reaction may have come out so quick (almost before you could think to do differently), because you have been "programmed" to react that way for so long, but if you'll begin to put something else in your heart continuously (God's Word), you'll begin to speak and act differently. The more time you spend with someone, the more you become like them. That's why the experts say, and it is even obvious by observation, that the longer a married couple stays together and spend time interacting together, the more they become like each other. The more time you spend talking and listening to your heavenly Father, renewing your mind in His Word, meditating it, speaking it, and choosing to obey it regardless of how you feel, you'll become like Him. And He is not angry, depressed or fearful!

Being honest with yourself regarding the desire to change brings about the beginning of your freedom. The biggest thing you must realize is that *you* must desire to change. Family and friends can want you to change, but until *you* want to be free, and *you* want to live this love-filled, peace-filled, joy-filled life, "it ain't happenin'!" However, if you have continued to this section, I believe you do want change! Your family and friends will reap the benefits, but they cannot change you, or make you want to change. Only God and you can! God does deliver some instantly, but the majority of changes in my life have come from me planting the seed of God's Word in my heart, letting it take deep root, keeping the weeds out, and God doing His part, the part I can't do…the growth and production of fruit. See Mark 4:1–20, and 26–29.

I will address the following symptoms and give scriptures related to dealing with each one: sleep disturbance, withdrawal/isolation, anger, anxiety, depression, substance abuse, startle response, relationships, etc.

Sleep disturbance—The Lord has promised us a peaceful sleep. The soldier/veteran oftentimes will have interrupted sleep patterns caused by nightmares or just waking up during the night for various reasons. The soldier or veteran becomes very aware of his surroundings and the slightest noise will awaken him. This is very fresh for the soldier just returning home from combat, and can be a habit or pattern developed by the veteran who has been home for years, but suffered under the weight of PTSD. The interrupted sleep pattern, my belief, comes partly from the pulling of guard duty and being awakened in the night by an enemy attack, which set an internal clock. Your body will adjust to whatever routine you put it through. It doesn't matter what the reason, though, God's Word has promised us a peaceful sleep and we need to meditate on the scriptures listed at the end of this section. The other thing is to guard what's going in to your "ear gate" and "eye gate." Your ears and eyes are the gateways to your heart. One preacher put it this way: "Garbage in, garbage out." Jesus said, "Take heed what you hear…" (Mark 4:24) and Proverbs 4:23 says, "Keep thy heart with all diligence; for out of it are the issues of life." It's not wise to listen to music, read books, or watch movies (particularly about war) that produce fear, and stimulate negative emotions, which could, and usually do, provoke the occurrence of nightmares, or "night terrors." This is especially important right before bed. Rather, prior to retiring for the night, read and meditate on God's Word and/or go to sleep with a peaceful worship CD. You can set the atmosphere. Here's the "engrafted Word that is able to save (heal, deliver, rescue, preserve, keep, and make whole) your soul." (James 1:21)

Scriptures:

Psalms 3:5 "I laid me down and slept; I awaked; for the *Lord* sustained me."

Psalms 4:8 "I will both lay me down in peace, and sleep: for thou, *Lord*, only makes me dwell in safety."

Psalms 127:2 "It is vain for you to rise up early, to sit up late, to eat the bread of sorrows: for so He giveth His beloved sleep."

Proverbs 3:24 "When thou liest down, thou shalt not be afraid: yea, thou shalt lie down, and thy sleep shall be sweet."

Withdrawal/isolation—"Through desire a man, having separated himself, seeketh and intermeddleth with all wisdom." (Proverbs 18:1) From the beginning God never intended for man to be alone. We can see this first in Genesis 2:18, where God said "And the *Lord* God said, It is not good that the man should be alone; I will make him an help meet for him." God gave Adam a most precious gift, in creating Eve. She would be there for him and him for her. I wouldn't be where I am today without the two most important relationships in my life...my relationship with God, and my relationship with Mary. God knew it was not good for man to be alone; that he would need a companion, a friend, and a lover. He never intended man to withdraw from society, isolate himself and become a recluse.

As a Christian we are told not to forsake the assembling of ourselves together, as sisters and brothers, even more so as the Day of the Lord approaches. (Hebrews 10:25) I believe this is because of the perilous times coming on the earth that Paul speaks of in II Timothy 3:1, and the darkness that shall cover the earth, gross darkness the people," prophesied by Isaiah, in chapter 60, verse 2. We need each other! We need to be with our brothers and sisters in Christ to serve them, help them, encourage them, comfort them, exhort or warn them, correct them, instruct them, etc., and be there to receive those things from them, as well. It is one avenue that God uses to strengthen us. People that choose to withdraw and isolate themselves will find themselves prey to the devil and the death and darkness he dwells in. These people become weak, spiritually. It's a dangerous place to be in. Even in the animal kingdom, you find animals that stray away from the herd, off all alone, are "easy prey" to their predators. There is a "safety," if you will, in numbers. The whole herd together is stronger in an attack from the enemy, than any of them standing alone. Surely, we are smarter than the animals!

God commands His blessing where people are united in the love of God. "Behold, how good and pleasant it is for brethren to dwell together in unity! It is like the precious ointment upon the head, that ran down upon the beard, even Aaron's beard: that went down to the skirts of his garments; As the dew of Hermon, and as the dew that descended upon the mountains of Zion: for *there* the *Lord* commanded the blessing, even life forevermore." (Psalms 133:1–3) We so need the encouragement and correction of our brothers and sisters in the Lord. It keeps us accountable and out of deception. Proverbs 27:17 says, "Iron sharpeneth iron; so a man sharpeneth the countenance of his friend."

We can see how Jesus sent His followers out in twos. "After these things the Lord appointed other seventy also, and sent them two and two before His face into every city and place, whither he himself would come." (Luke 10:1) Jesus knew the importance of agreement and what the disciples would face, so he sent them in pairs for strength and support. Matthew 18:18, 19 says "Verily I say unto you, Whatsoever ye shall bind on earth shall be bound in heaven: and whatsoever ye shall loose on earth shall be loosed in heaven." "Again I say unto you, That if two of you shall agree on earth as touching any thing that they shall ask, it shall be done for them of my Father which is in heaven." Solomon writes in Ecclesiastes 4:9–12, "Two are better than one; because they have a good reward for their labour. For if they fall, the one will lift up his fellow: but woe to him that is alone when he falleth; for he hath not another to help him up. Again, if two lie together, then they have heat: but how can one be warm alone? And if one prevail against him, two shall withstand him; and a threefold cord is not quickly broken." The person who isolates himself will give place to negative thought patterns and when meditating on them will fall into a deeper depression. Regardless of what anti-depressant you may be on, if you continue negative thought patterns you will be depressed. Change the way you think, get out, get some sunshine, enjoy some good fellowship with other believers, and reach out and help someone else. Get your mind off of *you*!

None of this, however, negates the wonderful experience of getting away by yourself, and spending time alone in fasting, prayer and the Word, with the Lord. This is a good thing! But even Jesus came out of that private, quiet time with His Father alone, to fellowship with and minister to his disciples (best friends and followers) and to crowds of people he didn't even know. His time with His Father gave Him the comfort and strength He needed for the task ahead, and to give of Himself the way He did. After all, He was God in a human body, and possessed a soul. He needed to be strengthened just like you and me.

You must also know that I'm certainly not advocating that you can never be alone. I'm specifically dealing with the desire in these soldiers/veterans to withdraw and isolate themselves completely from society. And there are some that do it!

Emotion based actions (anger, depression, anxiety, fear, grief, etc.)—Most counselors would tell their clients the following: You have an event occur, a thought comes, you have physiological signs, and then a behavior whether positive or negative. They will boldly tell you that the response to the event is totally in your hands. I personally believe there is a lot of error in "psychology training," because it is education that totally leaves out the power of God in a person's life, however, in this matter, I do believe they speak partial truth. They are basically trying to destroy the "victim mentality" in that person, and make them responsible for their own actions. Even though there may be a minority of "secular" counselors that teach differently, promoting the blaming of every one else in a person's life for their behavior, I personally, was not around "that crowd." Even the ones I worked with that weren't Christians did not hold to that vain of thinking. The biggest difference between a Christian counselor and a "secular" counselor is that the Christian counselor believes the Holy Spirit is there to help you in your weaknesses

(Romans 8:26), and that you can do all things through *Christ* (the Anointed One and His anointing), who strengthens you (Philippians 4:13). Most "secular" counselors believe you just make a decision on your own to behave correctly, that you have the power within you, apart from God, to be good, or do the right thing, that humans are "basically good." We know this is a lie. The Bible tells us that there are "none good, no not one" (Psalms 14:1 and Romans 3:10). Although the will is a very powerful thing, and this, indeed, can be done through hard work and struggle, how much easier it is to make a right decision and respond correctly by leaning on the grace of the One who gives you all the strength, power and ability you need to do what He would do. "For it is *God* which worketh in you both to will and to do of His good pleasure" (Philippians 2:13). It goes way beyond "will power," my friend! It is supernatural intervention of the best and highest kind…the kind that only comes from God alone. God says He not only gave you the power to do His will when you became His, but He gave you the "want to." That all happened in your spirit. That's why a part of you wants so bad to behave right. And, He keeps working this cycle of, what I call, "the want to and power to do," in your soul, your whole life on earth, as you abide in His Word and let His Word abide in you. This does not mean you don't exercise your human will. You do set your will in motion with a decision to obey God's Word instead of what you feel like doing right then, but once you make that decision, all of Heaven comes to back you up, and empower you to behave in the right way.

You may not be able to control the event, (what happens while you're driving, in the checkout line, etc.) but you can control the thoughts. "For though we walk in the flesh, we do not war after the flesh: (For the weapons of our warfare are not carnal, but mighty through God to the pulling down of strongholds;) Casting down imaginations, and every high thing that exalteth itself against the knowledge of God, and bringing into captivity every thought to the obedience of Christ; (II Corinthians 10:3–5) Philippians 4:8, tells us "Finally, brethren, whatsoever things are true, whatsoever things are honest, whatsoever things are just, whatsoever things are pure, whatsoever things are lovely, whatsoever things are of good report; and if there be any virtue, and if there be any praise, think on these things." God does not tell us to do something that He hasn't and doesn't empower us to do. A person who is Word minded gets Word results. Isaiah 26:3 tells us, "Thou wilt keep him in perfect peace, whose mind is stayed on thee: because he trusteth in thee." Romans 8:6 reveals to us that, "To be carnally minded is death; but to be spiritually minded is life and peace." "Carnally minded" is "earthly minded," or "of the five physical senses," or minding the things of the flesh (what you can see, taste, hear, smell and feel.) Spiritually minded is "Word minded," or your mind on the Word. Jesus said, in John 6:63, "...the words that I speak unto you, they are spirit, and they are life."

Another key in dealing with this area is your love walk. I Corinthians 13:4–8 tells us what "walking in love" entails. "Charity suffereth long, and is kind; charity envieth not; charity vaunteth not itself, is not puffed up, doeth not behave itself unseemly, seeketh not her own, is not easily provoked, thinketh no evil; Rejoiceth not in iniquity, but rejoiceth in the truth; Beareth all things, believeth all things, hopeth all things, endureth all things. Charity never faileth." When you walk in love you won't be seeking self-gratification. Rather, you will put others first. It is time to change your thinking that everyone is "out to get you." This thinking can come from memories of being surrounded by the enemy in war, or from a feeling of being "ripped off" because of the war, or since you've come home. In that case, you may have to get to a root of unforgiveness, bitterness and resentment, but even unforgiveness is rooted in fear. No matter how you look at it, and regardless of the root cause of the fear, that thought, which has now become a stronghold in your life is a fear-based thought, not a love-based thought. That makes it a lie of Satan...to be refused, rejected, renounced, rebuked and resisted with the truth. Everyone is not out to get you. Even if the whole world was, God isn't, so that's not everyone! Receiving a revelation of God's love for you is essential. "Perfect love casteth out fear." (I John 4:18) The Word says that God is for you, and if God be for you, who can be against you? And, even if every human being on earth around you was against you, the Word says, "The *Lord* is my light and my salvation; whom shall I fear? The *Lord* is the strength of my life; of whom shall I be afraid?" (Psalm 27:1) And Psalm, chapter 3, verses 1 and 3 says, "*Lord*, how are they increased that trouble me! Many are they that rise up against me. But thou, O *Lord*, art a shield for me; my glory, and the lifter of mine head." Verse 6 goes on to say, "I will not be afraid of ten thousands of people, that have set themselves against me round about." It is time for you to face your fears. And unless you are still in the war, surrounded by the enemy, I doubt that this is true. It's time to start crying, "search my heart, O God," and find out what's going on with you that causes you to see things this way. Maybe you're hanging out in all the wrong places and in all the wrong circles. Maybe the fear in your own heart of being "ripped off" again is drawing those kinds of people to you. Maybe you need to forgive someone, but most likely, this has become a "figment of your imagination," started by one little lie you bought, hook, line, and sinker, somewhere in your past. If you seek God with all your heart, you will find Him. He will not keep you in the dark. The entrance of His Word brings light. He will uncover every hidden thing and bring it out into the open, where you can see it for what it is, and repent (turn around; go the other way). At the very least, none of this kind of thinking has anything to do with how you should treat people who are not treating you right. Matthew, chapter 5 has plenty of instructions to us about how to treat our "enemies." (This is not speaking of war situations.) In war, as a trained soldier to defend your country and the cause of your country, it is highly probable that you may be the one to have to kill your enemy. Jesus was dealing with "enemies" on a personal level, as we live. God addresses the job and authority of military officials, police officers, rulers of the land, etc., in Romans, chapter 13. This is a whole other subject...one I will not get into in this writing. It's not the purpose of this book...maybe another book, for another time.

There are multitudes of scriptures that will help you conquer anxiety, depression, anger, etc. Even the medical world has caught up with God's Word in their discovery of the health benefits of laughter. God said it a long time ago, when He inspired Solomon to write, "A merry heart doeth good like a medicine but a contrite spirit dries the bones." (Proverbs 17:22). And, "A sound heart is the life of the flesh: but envy the rottenness of the bones." (Proverbs 14:30) A sound heart is a calm and undisturbed one, void of turmoil, and envy can include anger. Is it any wonder that so many who suffer with depression also have joint related illnesses? Jesus bore your sin, your sorrow, your grief, your distress, your weakness, your pain, and your sickness. The chastisement of your peace was upon Him. (Isaiah 53:4, 5) He bore it so you don't have to. You can choose peace today. You can choose joy today. You can choose health today, mental, emotional and physical. It's yours in Christ Jesus. Anxiety, which, real simply, is worry, can and will cause depression. "Heaviness in the heart of man maketh it stoop: but a good word maketh it glad." (Proverbs 12:25) It is all just other names for fear. You might say, "Brother Mike, I don't worry." Well, let's just see. Do you wake up in the morning and go to bed at night thinking on how you're going to pay your bills? Do you spend much of your time thinking on the economy, interest rates, the unemployment rates and gas and food prices, wondering just how you're going to make it if it all keeps rising? Do you spend all of your time thinking about that little symptom in your body that the doctors just can't seem to figure out, wondering if it might be diabetes, heart problems or cancer? Or how about those symptoms that the doctors have diagnosed? Do you spend your time thinking on whether you will live or die? Do you spend most of your time thinking about the pain, and just how to relieve it, and if you relieve it with pain medication, what will the damage be to your body in the long run? Do you spend your day thinking about that last fight you and your spouse just had, what you wish you would have said, what you're going to say the next time that subject gets brought up again? Do you spend the majority of your time thinking about all the recent natural disasters, terrorist attacks, and plagues recently happening in the earth? Do you spend all your time thinking about what's going to transpire in Iraq, how many more soldiers will die, and whether or not it's all worth it? There are thousands of other things people worry about, regarding children, parents, spouses, jobs, finances and yes, even vacations. These are just a few, but if you answered yes to any of these, you have just told me that you worry. All worry is, is meditating on negative circumstances. Jesus told us not to let our hearts be troubled, neither let them be afraid, and that in the world we would have tribulation, but to be of good cheer, because He had overcome the world (John 14:1, 27 and John 16:33). Philippians 4:6 tells us not to be anxious for anything. Proverbs 15:15 says, "All the days of the afflicted are evil: but he that is of a merry heart hath a continual feast." Jesus certainly told us not to worry about our life, what we would wear, what we would eat, and about the horrible things that are coming upon the earth in the last days, that it wouldn't add one cubit of stature to us. It wouldn't help a bit, in my language! He told us to seek first the kingdom of God and everything we needed would be added to us. Replace all those "worry-thoughts" with the Word of God! Sing and praise your God! You can praise your way out of depression! God's Word tells us to put on the "garment of praise" for the spirit of heaviness (Isaiah 61:3). Praise shuts up the mouth of the enemy...stills the avenger, among other things. (Psalm 8:2)

If you're dealing with "panic attacks," spend time praying in tongues throughout the day. It will refresh you. (Isaiah 28:11, 12) It will build you up in your most holy faith (Jude 20 and I Corinthians 14:4). The Holy Spirit will help your weakness (Romans 8:26). He will strengthen you (Isaiah 40:29–31). You will be praying God's perfect will in that situation (Romans 8:27). And you're giving thanks well (I Corinthians 14:17). Spend time praising, thanking and worshipping God. The righteous sing and rejoice (Proverbs 29:6). The Psalms are full of exhortations to sing to the Lord and praise Him, right in the midst of the worst circumstances and your darkest hour. Dance before Him (Psalms 149:3 and 150:4). *Shout* unto God with a voice of triumph! (Psalms 47:1). This is exactly what Paul and Silas did sitting in a nasty, dirty dungeon with their feet and hands in stocks (Acts 16:19–36). Suddenly there was an earthquake and the prison doors were opened. Paul and Silas' shackles were unfastened. Paul and Silas stayed around to lead the jailer and his household to the Lord, but the next day, the authorities released them and let them go. God was surrounding them with "songs of deliverance," and that's exactly what happened. "Thou are my hiding place; thou shalt preserve me from trouble; thou shalt compass me about with songs of deliverance. Selah" (Psalms 32:7).

Panic attacks often occur when people leave their homes, though they can even occur at home. My wife dealt with these during a difficult time in our lives, mostly when she would leave home, until she found the scriptures in Psalms 121:7, 8, "The *Lord* shall preserve thee from all evil: he shall preserve thy soul. The *Lord* shall preserve thy going out and thy coming in from this time forth, and even forevermore." When she saw that, she said, "That is mine!" She claimed it and wrote it on our magnetic board on the refrigerator. She wrote it on 3x5 cards and taped them on the bathroom mirror, above the nightstand on the wall on her side of the bed, on the dash of the car, and even wrote it on her hand. She placed that Word everywhere she knew to put it, to help her to meditate it and speak it. She also clung to "I can do all things through Christ which strengtheneth me" (Philippians 4:13). It wasn't very long before she was free, applying the wonderful medicine of God's Word. They are a thing of the past for her. The Word of God will work for you, too, if you'll crave it, pursue it, delight in it, meditate in it, study it, believe and receive it for yourself and speak it all day long (Psalms 1). Look at the Bible study notes on Conquering Your Emotions and Anger. Hide the Word in the midst of your heart, make a choice to believe it and speak it until you receive God's revelation on these matters, and then keep yourself in remembrance of them. Make a journal of all the good things God does for you, no matter how little they seem, and go back from time to time, reminding yourself of them. Letting Jesus live His life through you is a daily choice. Paul said, "I die daily," meaning he crucified his flesh daily. Every day Paul reckoned himself alive to God and dead to sin (I Corinthians 15:31, Romans 6:11, 8:13, and Galatians 5:24). And, don't forget that keeping your mind stayed on the Lord keeps you in perfect peace (Isaiah 26:3). It's His promise to you. Sometimes the mental torment and emotions are so strong you can't even think straight enough to speak God's Word. In those times, just call on His name. Just say the name of Jesus. He'll come to your rescue every time (Acts 2:21). He's an ever-present help in the time of trouble (Psalms 46:1). His grace will deliver you. I also urge you to look the scriptures up in several different translations (Amplified, New Living, NIV, Message, Moffits, etc.). It is very helpful and enlightening.

Substance abuse (drugs or alcohol)—As mentioned previously in Chapter IV, the GI may turn to drugs/alcohol as a way of coping or emotional numbing during the war and/or while home on leave. The soldier returns home and the memories are still there. He remembers that the drugs/alcohol numbed the pain during his war experience, and certainly seemed to make him forget the pain and "make him feel good" while home on leave, so why not now. He continues using the drugs/alcohol at first, to fall asleep at night (self-medication) and eventually to start the day. The addictive pattern is soon controlling his life and affects everyone around him. These soldiers/veterans may find themselves missing work, losing jobs, being separated or divorced, imprisoned, etc. They look for help and attend a substance abuse program, which seems to work for a time, and may even be enough for some, in the sense of "never touching it again." I wouldn't call them free, because they are taught that once they are an alcoholic or drug addict, they will always be an alcoholic or drug addict. This is not freedom, my friend. With that kind of thinking, fear will always be lurking in the background that you might take it up again. I won't say that you are not most definitely "better," if you never touch the stuff again. But for many, that fear actually draws the thing right back to them. The devil will see to that, especially if you are a believer. You run into an old drinking buddy, you have an argument at work or home and feel rejected. You remember the anniversary of a friend's death, etc. and you return to the addictive behavior. It is the same way you always dealt with these things, using the drugs or alcohol to escape, numb the pain and feel better. This will continue until the root issue is dealt with, whether combat-related, or otherwise. Even once you've dealt with the root cause (anger, unforgiveness, escape, etc.) of your drug/alcohol abuse, opportunities will continue to surface until you've said no to that kind of behavior so many times the devil gives up on you. You have to outlast him. Wear him out. Don't ever let him wear you out. He will wait for a time when you are "weaker" and more vulnerable to tempt you again, but that's the importance of staying in close fellowship with God, keeping an active prayer life, being involved with believers (church), and abiding in the Word of God. You keep yourself strong through your relationship with God and relationships with other strong believers. Give the devil no place (Ephesians 4:27). Remember I Corinthians 10:3–5, and take your rightful authority, casting down those vain imaginations. The devil would like nothing more than to keep you in bondage and not walking in the freedom Jesus provided. It is time to stop blaming things and other people, institutions, or God for your own choices that created the problem(s) you have found yourself in. Proverbs 19:3 says, "The foolishness of man perverteth his way: and his heart fretteth against the *Lord*." If you don't like the way you're living, let the Lord change it! And begin by taking responsibility for your own choices.

Let's look at some scriptures and pay special attention to how drunkenness affects your life.

Proverbs 20:1 "Wine is a mocker, strong drink is raging: and whosoever is deceived thereby is not wise."

Proverbs 23:29–35) "Who hath woe? Who hath sorrow? Who hath contentions? Who hath babblings? Who hath wounds without cause? Who hath redness of eyes? 30) They that tarry long at the wine; they that go to seek mixed wine. 31) Look not thou upon the wine when it is red, when it giveth his colour in the cup, when it moveth itself aright. 32) At the last it biteth like a serpent, and stingeth like an adder. 33) Thine eyes shall behold strange women, and thine heart shall utter perverse things. 34) Yea, thou shalt be as he that lieth down in the midst of the sea or as he that lieth upon the top of a mast. 35) They have stricken me, shalt thou say, and I was not sick; they have beaten me, and I felt it not: when shall I awake? I will seek it yet again.

Proverbs 31:4–5) "It is not for kings, O Lemuel, It is not for kings to drink wine; Nor for princes strong drink: 5) Lest they drink and forget the law, and pervert the judgment of any of the afflicted."

Hosea 4:11 "Whoredom and wine, and new wine take away the heart." Another translation says, "enslaves the heart." Interesting...

Ephesians. 5:18 "And be not be drunk with wine, wherein is excess; but be filled with the Spirit;"

Revelation 1:6 "And hath made us kings and priests unto God and his Father; to Him be glory and dominion for ever and ever. Amen." In my opinion, it is just better for "kings and priests," which we are (Jesus made us these) to stay away from alcohol. It is a proven fact that even one drink of wine/strong drink destroys brain cells, and impairs clear thinking, even if you think not. And, at the very least, why take the chance of where one drink might take you? I've never seen alcohol do anything good for anybody, but I have seen it bring plenty of destruction to those who use it themselves, and their families.

The scriptures point out that the person given to wine and strong drink are brawlers, womanizers, and not wise. Is this someone you want to be? What has the addictive behavior cost you (finances, relationships, employment, imprisonment, etc)? Remember Psalms 107:20 says, "He sent His word and healed them, and delivered them from their destructions." His Word will heal and deliver you. The scriptures are also clear that wine and strong drink aren't for kings, or princes (rulers), of which we are when we become the Lord's. Proverbs 31:3 tells us not to give your strength to *that* which ruins and destroys kings, and in the very next verse, Solomon says not to give yourself to wine and strong drink. Over-consumption of alcohol leads to ruin and destruction.

Startle response: A backfire, bursting balloon, or sudden and unexpected loud noise may startle you. The reaction is usually hit the ground or take cover. The noise can't be avoided but the action can be controlled. The noise may bring back to mind a rocket attack bombing, fire fight, etc. but the reaction is fear-based. While in a combat area it saved your life, but you aren't in a combat zone now. I dealt with this the first time I went to an Air Force football game when the jets went over the stadium so low. I "hit the deck," with my friend laughing hysterically. I can laugh about it now, but it wasn't very funny then. I also experienced it during a 21-gun salute, firework displays, sonic booms, extremely loud thunder, and even our grandsons popping their birthday balloons. "God hath not given us the spirit of fear; but of power, and of love, and of a sound mind" (II Timothy 1:7). Reactions are controlled by our thoughts, so renewing your mind with this truth through meditation is essential. Personalize it and say, "God has not given *me* the spirit of fear. I have power. I have love. I have a sound mind. Jesus has freed me from fear. You can go back to the section on Emotions, in this chapter, if you would like more scriptures on your freedom from fear, and on the peace of God. There is nothing like His peace!

Relationship issues—Relationships are built on trust and love toward each other. So often the ability to trust is changed while in the combat area, because in the wars fought these days, you never know who your enemy might be. Oftentimes the nationals, who are supposed to be on your side, will run under fire or the civilian hired to work is really an enemy sympathizer checking out your LZ and perimeter. These soldiers become suspicious of everyone around them and continually have their guard up. This is also common amongst police officers, because of the nature of their work. This can carry over into the marriage and it is oftentimes difficult to trust the spouse. This lack of trust and inability to communicate openly leads to many divorces among combat soldiers and veterans. Refusing to deal with it causes them to eventually become paranoid and think that everyone is out to get them. (Go back to the third paragraph in the section on Emotions). It is important that you meditate on the love of God. (I Corinthians 13:4–8). As you meditate on these and nearly the entire book of I John, you will begin putting others first. Take even the first sentence of I Corinthians 4:4, "Love is patient," and dwell on it. Say it over and over to yourself, especially in a situation where you find yourself becoming impatient. God's power (grace) will come to you to obey it. And unless you're determined to fight or resist God, you find it easy to obey, and the peace of God comes. It's awesome! God doesn't make you obey, but gives you all the power you need to obey. Romans 13:8 says, "Owe no man any thing, but to love one another…" When you walk in God's kind of love, you won't want to hurt your spouse (in word or in deed). Remember, forget those things which are behind. Let the past be the past. Whatever has happened in the past is water under the bridge. With a sincere heart, ask and receive forgiveness and move on.

Survivor's guilt will be addressed in the next chapter related to commonly asked questions. In the beginning of this section I mentioned how the therapist would use cognitive and behavioral therapy. They teach that changing your thinking will change your behavior. This is a truth, but not the whole Truth. At best, it is a struggle in the natural. It is void of the power of God to change a life by His Spirit and through His Word. "…receive with meekness the engrafted word, which is able to save your souls" (James 1:21). "The law of the *Lord* is perfect, converting the soul: the testimony of the *Lord* is sure, making wise the simple" (Psalms 19:7). It is true that "as a man thinks in his heart, so is he" (Proverbs 18:21), however one cannot take one scripture, isolate it and build an entire doctrine on it. Cognitive and behavioral therapy cannot save your soul and make you a free man. Receiving Jesus will! He gives you a new heart, a new spirit, one that wants to do right, no matter what kind of mess your choices have put you in. The born again believer has a new spirit and is a new creation. Old things are passed away. Behold, all things have become new. The believer must meditate on the Word to renew their mind. The renewed mind will transform you, and change the way you react to any situation that may arise. The Holy Spirit is ever present with you to help you. I cannot emphasize enough, the importance of honesty when receiving your healing. Some people will be quick to blame the last tragedy, such as a combat situation, but the root issue may go back to childhood. Blessed are the pure in heart (Matthew 5:8). Be open and forgive *all* that may have hurt you. If you stumble, remember I John 1:9, confess it and move on.

Chapter Seven: Questions/Thoughts

This section will be dedicated to answering various questions or thoughts the soldier/veteran, himself, might have. I realize there are numerous questions and I couldn't begin to list them all, although I will address some of the most frequently asked of me over the years.

* * *

"Those who were killed are the "lucky ones." They don't have to deal with the mental torment."—This statement, in one sense is true, for the Christian, but most definitely not for the one who has rejected Jesus Christ as Savior and Lord. Those who knew Jesus as their Lord and Savior are in heaven rejoicing because of their belief in and on the Lord Jesus Christ (John 3:16, Romans 10:9, 10 and Acts). And so, yes, in that respect, they have experienced the fullness of their reward, and the ultimate healing and deliverance that God in His heaven brings. We can and do most certainly celebrate their "home-going," and look forward to seeing them again...soon. However, even though they are in heaven rejoicing, through a war that God never ordained, their families were robbed of living out a full life with their loved ones on the earth, and they, themselves, were robbed of fulfilling all that God wanted them to accomplish on the earth. Satan stole from them (John 10:10). Wars come from the lust and strivings of men (James 4:1–3). God has promised every one of us a long life on the earth (Psalms 91:16). This would be a bare minimum of 70 healthy and strong years, in my opinion, and I believe the scripture bares this out (Psalm 90:10). Each and every one that were killed had gifts, talents, a God-given plan and purpose, an assignment, if you will, and it was thwarted and short-circuited...aborted. However, those who died didn't die in vain, because they gave their lives in service to God and our country. It needs to be shouted from the housetops! Freedom isn't free!! The freedom America has experienced for over 200 years cost many soldiers their lives. Our ultimate freedom from sin and its penalty cost Jesus Christ His life on the cross!! It is up to us, the ones still alive, to "pick up our cross and follow Jesus." We must continue on, honor God, and give back to society in whatever He tells us and shows us to do, in honor of and remembering those who gave their life. One of the most painful things to my soul is when tragedy strikes and the news media points out it was a soldier or veteran (Vietnam/Persian Gulf). I guarantee this soldier/veteran was crying out for help at some point. Most likely his/her problems were evident, but no one around him/her were discerning enough to recognize the symptoms or have enough knowledge of God to reach them with the gospel. This is why the Word of God must spread in this land and abroad through every avenue of media possible (books, magazines, radio, television, the movie theater screen, preachers on the streets, preachers in the churches, preachers to the masses, and one-on-one ministry).

* * *

"I'll never forgive them" (government, society, protesters, etc.).—This has been covered in detail in Chapter V and in the Bible study notes on forgiveness. Just go back and refresh your soul.

* * *

"The government owes me."—This is a lie that many veterans have bought into. Vietnam veterans, in particular, often comment on not having any "welcome home parades" and being met by hostile and some times crude, rude and violent protestors upon their return. Even so, the government doesn't owe you anything. If you'll remember back to either your draft notice or enlistment contract, no where was there a clause, promising a parade, no protestors...not even a promise of even coming home alive. Remember you were answering the call to serve your country. Many are killed or wounded during our country's military involvement and we should be choosing and developing a thankful heart to God for what our country does to help and serve the veteran. All veterans have the same opportunities upon discharge from the armed forces in this country. They are entitled to the GI Bill for education, for buying a home, and medical assistance, just to name a few. The opportunities are there. However, the veteran must pursue these things. There are numerous veterans' service organizations like the VFW, DAV, PVA, American Legion, VVA and BVA to help the veteran's receive benefits rightly awarded to them. Many veterans are ignorant of what belongs to them (what they are entitled to), and some are just plain unwilling to apply because of inner contempt and anger toward the country. In many countries, the wounded veterans of wars are left on streets begging for sustenance, and the bodies of the dead are left lying where they died to rot. No one comes to their loved one's homes to comfort them. Our government has been and still is very gracious to our veterans. That doesn't mean there isn't any room for improvement, but I don't know any thing on earth that meets the criteria for "perfection." Men run it and men are not perfect. There was and is only one Perfect One, the man Christ Jesus, who is God. Isaiah calls Him, "Wonderful, Counselor, Mighty God, the Everlasting Father." Do yourself a favor. Seek God and do some real soul-searching about all these matters. Let it go! For my Vietnam veteran comrades, it has been over thirty years since the end of the Vietnam Conflict (War). How long are you going to be miserable, bound and "in chains?" Freedom from the war within awaits you, my friend.

***

"Where was God during Vietnam?"—God was and is still on his throne and willing to answer anyone's cry for salvation (John 3:16). We live in a fallen, corrupt and depraved world in which bad decisions are made. Once a decision has been made there are always consequences (positive or negative). Our country's involvement in World War I, World War II, Korea, Vietnam, the Persian Gulf, Bosnia, Kosovo Afghanistan, and Iraq has affected many lives. There have been many good results from these wars and surely, some negative "fallout," or negative results from these wars. Freedom has never been free, my friend. Even your eternal salvation wasn't free. It cost Jesus Christ suffering beyond our comprehension and ultimately His life. Killing and wars has never been God's will or plan for mankind. Fallen man with a sin nature of pride, fear, greed, selfishness, unforgiveness, bitterness, resentments, jealousy and envy, malice and hatred have instituted war, not to mention the influence of demonic forces in the earth, that some are submitting to. God's perfect will is that all men be saved, all men be made free, all men love the Lord God with all their heart mind, soul and strength and all men love one another. *God is love!!!* From the beginning, it wasn't God's will or desire that evil come to anyone. And it certainly hasn't been His will for men and women to lose their lives in a war, children to lose their daddies and mommies, husbands to lose their wives, wives to lose their husbands, moms and dads to lose their sons, grandparents to lose their grandsons, etc., but rather that they would turn to Him and be saved. (Acts 2:21, Acts 4:12 and Romans 10:13) The word "saved" here is the Greek word, *sozo*, which is translated "rescued," "delivered," "healed," "preserved" and "made whole." Even in the Old Testament, the provision of God's protection for His people has always been available. (Psalms 91) However, even in the midst of our worst tragedies, that even though God is not the author of "killing, stealing and destroying," that has taken place, (see John 10:10), we can know, as believers and covenant children of His, that He loves us, He is with us and will never leave us helpless, abandon us, or forsake us. God will turn every tragedy into a triumph that will bring Him glory, if we will let Him. (II Corinthians 2:14) It was never God's will for Joseph to be thrown into a pit by his brothers and sold to the Egyptians as a slave. It was not God's will for him to be separated from his father and family and people for all those years, but "what Joseph's brothers meant for evil," God took and turned for Joseph's good. He turned Joseph's victimization into victory, not only for Joseph, but for his family and people as well. You can read the entire account of Joseph's life from Genesis 37-Genesis 50, but pay particular attention to Genesis 45:4–8, and Genesis 50:20. So don't be distressed, disheartened, or angry. Give your cares to God and trust Him to turn *your* tragedies into triumphs. Both Joseph and Job, as well as many others in the Bible, did this, and God restored all the years that "the locust had eaten, and more" (Joel 2:25, 26). Don't be deceived! *God is good...all the time!!!*

***

"Why was (insert name) killed or injured and not me?"—This is a tough question for many veterans to settle in their heart. Survivor guilt is probably one of the biggest issues that haunts the combat veteran still today. The answer to this question has several parts. The first part would entail what he believed while in the combat zone. Did he believe in his heart that he would survive or was his constant meditation on not returning home? Mark 11:23, 24 is the law of faith. It works all the time, whether to one's detriment or one's benefit. Fear is perverted or "twisted" faith. It is, in a sense, "faith" in and on all the wrong things. Fear draws the very thing one fears the most to him. It is a spiritual force (Job 3:24). Just as faith in God and His Word, is the vehicle that brings His precious Word and promises to pass in our lives, (the things we do want), fear draws the things we don't want. Remember, Proverbs 23:7 says, "As a man thinketh in his heart so is he." Secondly, what did he speak? "I'm not going to make it?" "I know my "luck" isn't going to last?" A soldier that is ignorant of the truths we've discussed in this book, usually makes numerous fear based statements prior to leaving to war. His meditation usually begins the second he is informed that he will be going to the battlefield. Words are containers of power. They charge the atmosphere with life or death, blessing or cursing. They fill the minds and hearts of the people speaking them and the hearts and minds of those who hear them. "Life and death are in the power of the tongue: and they that love it shall eat the fruit thereof" (Proverbs 18:21). These spoken words can open the door to attacks from the enemy, the devil (Satan), and all his demonic cohorts, though this does not mean that every attack against a believer is because of something he or she said. And many of the negative things going on in believer's lives have nothing to do with the devil. It's simply our own lack of wisdom, knowledge, understanding, discretion, discernment and prudence. We are believing a lie somewhere and not the Truth. Satan is a liar. He has been stripped. Jesus whipped him good! He is powerless. The only power is what men give him by yielding their hearts and minds to his lies. God's Word is forever settled in heaven and earth (Psalms 119:89 and Mark 13:31). Spiritual laws work for the believer and unbeliever alike. We are in more control of our destiny than even most Christians believe, based on our decisions. "I call heaven and earth as witnesses today against you, that I have set before you life and death, blessing and cursing; therefore (YOU) choose life, that both you and your descendants may live" (Deuteronomy 30:19). The third part is prayer. We have no idea who may have been praying for us while in the combat zone. The Holy Spirit could have spoken to a believer to pray at a particular time and their prayer brought deliverance from a tragedy (firefight, ambush, chopper crash, mine, etc.).

***

"Will this mental torment ever stop?" *Yes! Yes! Yes!* As a believer you can expect complete freedom, healing and deliverance through the Word of God (Psalm 107:20). God cannot lie. He's not a man that He should lie (Numbers 23:19, Titus 1:2). But, you must read or hear His Word in order to know what He has promised. Your Bible will not help you at all sitting on your coffee table, nightstand or bookshelf. Open it, study it, meditate in it and on it and renew your mind to who God really is. *God is love!* Find out who you are in Him. (Christ). Quit trying to change! Stop struggling in the arm of the flesh (your own strength) and trust in the arm of the Lord. (Psalm 44:3) Let His Word change you!!! Jesus has paid the price. He purchased your redemption, salvation and freedom from all that binds and holds you back with His very life. His blood was the "cash." And now He turns to you and says, "Here, Mike." "Here, Bob." "Here, Mary." "It's yours. Go ahead. Take it. Freely receive, and then go tell somebody else what I have done for you." " Jesus Christ is the same yesterday, today, and forever" (Hebrews 13:8). What Jesus did while on earth, He is still doing today, but we must believe. That's our part. We believe. And what you're believing, you are speaking, so believe the Word! Jesus told us that out of the abundance of our heart, our mouth speaks (Matthew 12:34). Paul said, "we believe, therefore, we speak" (II Corinthians 4:13). Faith has a voice. Remember, you are either blessing your life and the lives of others with your words, or cursing them; healing them or destroying them. James, chapter 3 makes all this very clear. The book of Proverbs is full of the wisdom of guarding our tongue, and speaking right things. Even Peter tells us that if we want to see good days and live a long life, to keep our lips from speaking guile (deceit, lies) (I Peter 3:10). But God is the performer! He watches over His Word to perform it (Jeremiah 1:12). So, trust Him, rely on Him, have confidence in Him and cling to Him! Fill your life with the presence of God and His Word, and you can't be anything but changed into His image more and more. You'll be changed from glory to glory!! It is God, Himself, who works in you to do His good pleasure (Philippians 2:13). His hand of love is extended, friend. Reach out and receive! God bless you!

(Review the Bible study notes on the tongue).

Chapter Eight: Bible Study Notes

I have added the following Bible study notes. These are teachings heard over the years after my salvation in 1979 that helped me receive my freedom. I reviewed many teaching series and prepared notes for my monthly veteran's Bible study. The lessons were designed for new believers and with the idea of giving the "simple gospel message" to help fellow veterans overcome hidden issues by meditating on God's Word. Each lesson is easy to understand and full of scriptures that will produce life for the reader. So grab your Bible and look up each scripture for yourself and meditate on it. Never just believe it when a person says, "the Bible says…" and then they quote a scripture. Look it up for yourself. Enjoy your time in the scriptures and as III John 2 says, "Beloved, I wish above all things that thou mayest prosper and be in health, even as thou soul prospereth."

1 Salvation

The first step to deliverance from the past is believing in the Lord Jesus. The following are the scripture references for salvation. Remember, Romans 10:9, 10 says to believe and confess. As stated before God looks at the heart and if you truly mean it from your heart when praying then you are saved.

I have done my own paraphrasing of the King James scriptures in all my Bible study notes for simpler reading.

Salvation Scriptures:

John 3:3 Jesus answered and said to him, "Most assuredly, I say to you, unless one is born again, he cannot see the kingdom of God."

John 3:16 God so loved the world that he gave His only begotten Son, that whoever believes in Him shall not perish but have everlasting life.

John 14:6 I am the way, truth and the life. No one comes to the Father but through me.

Romans 3:23 All have sinned and come short of the glory of God.

Romans 6:23 The wages of sin is death, but the gift of God is eternal life.

Romans 10:9–10 That if you confess with your mouth the *Lord* Jesus and believe in your heart that God has raised Him from the dead, you will be saved. For with the heart one believes unto righteousness, and with the mouth confession is made unto salvation.

Ephesians 2:8–9 For grace you have been saved through faith, and that not of yourselves; it is the gift of God, not of works, lest anyone should boast.

2 Baptism in the Holy Spirit

The baptism in the Holy Spirit is what gives us the power to be overcomers. Like our salvation, the baptism of the Holy Spirit is a free gift which is received from God. In Matthew 3:11, Mark 1:8, and Luke 3:16 John the Baptist tells us that he baptizes in water but there will be someone who baptizes with fire. In Matthew 4 we see where Jesus was water baptized and the Holy Spirit descended on Him like a dove. He was then led into the wilderness and tempted by the devil. It was the Holy Spirit and the Word of God that brought His deliverance from each temptation. This same power is available to us as believers. Jesus told His disciples that the Father would send the Comforter to teach, lead, and guide them in John 14:26. In John 20:21–22, Jesus told the disciples to receive the Holy Ghost. Then in Acts 1:4–8 He told them to tarry in Jerusalem until they received the Holy Spirit. As we continue in Acts 2:1–2, we see where the 120 were gathered in the upper room and the Holy Spirit came upon them like a rushing wind, filling them with the Holy Spirit. They spoke in other tongues and a boldness came on them. Continuing through Acts, we can see where the disciple asked the new believers if they had received the Holy Spirit since they believed (Acts 8:14–17, 10:44–46, 11:16 and 19:1–6). The new believers weren't aware of any other baptism except John's water baptism. The disciples prayed and laid hands on them to receive the Holy Spirit and they spoke in tongues. The new believer, when baptized in the Holy Spirit, receives a prayer language, which is a "hot line" to God. Jude 20 tells us that praying in the spirit builds up your most holy faith and Romans 8:26 tells us that praying in the spirit helps our infirmities. I Corinthians 12:1–10 lists the gifts of the Spirit, which a person can operate in. The baptism of the Holy Spirit isn't something to take lightly. As a believer we should want to have everything available to us and operate in the same power as the early believers. Remember that in Mark 16:15, Jesus said these signs shall follow the believer; they shall speak in other tongues…Are you a believer? Then you should be speaking in other tongues and doing the other things listed in Mark 16, casting out devils, healing the sick.

3 Grace (God's Unmerited Favor)

We have seen how salvation comes by grace through faith, a gift of God (Ephesians 2:8–9). Most people believe that once we are saved by grace, that we must then perform to receive anything from God. God isn't withholding any blessings from us, but rather our thinking is the hindrance. "As a man thinketh in his heart so is he (Proverbs 23:7). James 2:10 says that if you keep the whole law but offend in one point you become guilty of all. Colossians 2:6 says, As you have therefore received Christ Jesus the Lord so walk ye in Him. This simply means that if you put your faith in God's grace for salvation then continue to walk in that grace. Your holiness does not make God love you, but rather the lack of holiness will make you love God less. God loved us when we were still sinners and sent His Son (John 3:16, 17).

All error of scriptures comes when you look away from what Jesus did. Jesus is our only righteousness and justification to God. Jesus is the author and finisher of your faith (Hebrews 12:2).

Salvation means forgiveness of sins, healing, deliverance, and prosperity. Gospel means the "good news." Romans 3:19, 20 tells that the law was given to provide the knowledge of sin. Hebrews 10:1 says that we should have no more consciousness of sin. Religion is just the opposite. It points out your sin rather than what Jesus has done. I Corinthians 15:56 The strength of sin is the law. The law was given to take away the deception that you were good enough. It was given to show you that a Savior was needed and that you could never attain on your own. Study Romans starting at 5:13 through chapter 7.

Romans 8:1 If you are feeling condemnation, then you are under the law and not grace.

Romans 3:19–22 points out the reason for the law. Blame is put directly on the person rather than passing the buck. Adam blamed Eve and then blamed God by saying, "it was that woman you gave me." Psychology today puts the blame everywhere except on the person. It comes down to taking responsibility. We can choose to be bitter or better.

Remember that God sees you righteous, holy, and pure. He sees you through Jesus and not yourself. You are created for God's pleasure (Revelations 4:11).

4 Faith

What is faith? Simple definition: Faith is your positive response to God's grace, independent of your effort. Biblical definition: "Now faith is the substance of things hoped for; the evidence of things not seen" (Hebrews 11:1). As we have read before, faith is a gift of God (Ephesians 2:8, 9) which was given to receive God's grace for our salvation. Everyone who is saved has the measure of faith (Romans 12:3). We can see in I Corinthians 12:9 that there is a special gift of faith given by the Holy Spirit. In Galatians 5:22 we see that faith is a fruit of the spirit. Romans 1:17 says, "the just shall live by faith." In Hebrews 11:6 it says "without faith it is impossible to please God." Can our faith be increased? Jesus, Himself, spoke of no faith, little faith, and great faith. Look at Romans 10:17 "Faith comes by hearing and hearing by the Word of God." I John 5:4 says, "This is the victory that overcomes the world, even our faith." "Faith without works is dead" James 2:19. The works are not unto salvation but rather works of your faith. True faith will always produce works (action). We must "believe that he is a rewarder of those who diligently seek Him" (Hebrews 11:6). Mark chapter five shows how desire and faith are different. The woman with the issue of blood was healed because of her faith, while the others thronging Jesus were desiring healing but didn't have the faith. They were going on the news of his healing power but never totally believed He could heal them. She not only believed and said, "if I but touch the hem of his garment, I will be healed," but she put action to her faith and belief. Look at Mark 11:23–24 and you will see how this principle worked in her life. II Corinthians 5:7 says "we walk by faith; not by sight." Human faith is believing in the physical senses (sight, touch, taste, smell, and hearing). When we get saved, we use God's faith (Hebrews 11:1). "The words that I speak unto you, they are spirit, and they are life." (John 6:63). To know what spiritual truth is, we must study the Word of God. The Word says to study to show thy self approved (II Timothy 2:15). Studying the Word renews your mind (Romans 12:2) and causes us to be spiritually (Word) minded rather than carnally (earthly, of this world) minded. As we study the Word, you will start applying your faith and using it like a muscle, to see God's promises come to pass in your life. Hebrews 10:23 says "Hold fast the profession of your faith without wavering, for He is faithful who has promised."

"Whatsoever is not of faith is sin" (Romans 14:23). Faith works by love (Galatians 5:6). We will look at love next, as a vital part of faith.

Let's look at I Corinthians Chapter 13 and I John chapter 4. These two chapters sum up how we should live our lives and why we have hindrances.

5 Love

Faith works by love (Galatians 5:6), so in this lesson we will look at God's kind of love. Jesus gave us a new commandment (John 13:34, 35). In this commandment He reveals that the world will know us because of our love one for another. Let's look at John 15:13. We know this is talking of Jesus and what He is about to do for the world at the cross. As a veteran we look at those who might have taken a bullet for us. Love one for another doesn't end on the battlefield. I

John 4:7 talks about God being love, and tells us that love is being perfected in us. Love is a fruit of the spirit (Galatians 5:22) just like faith, and we can grow or increase in our love. Romans 5:5 states, "The love of God is shed abroad in our hearts by the Holy Ghost." Look at Romans 13:8–11. We see that if we truly walk in love, the other commandments are fulfilled. When walking in love, we don't want to offend another in anyway. However, the Truth will always offend some. The first sign of salvation is that we love the brethren (I John 3:14, 15). It is difficult at times to show our love toward our family members, let alone someone else. I Thessalonians 3:12, 13 tells us that our love is to abound not only to our brothers and sisters in the Lord, but to those outside the church. We can't just think of ourselves, but rather we must look at the world through the eyes of Jesus. There are a lot of hurting people out there who need to know of Jesus' love and what He has done for them. We are His mouthpiece on the earth and should freely tell others what He has done in our lives (Luke 10:10). Walking in love, one toward another, perfects our holiness. When we aren't walking in love and have unforgiveness in our heart, we can see physical symptoms, high blood pressure, ulcers, rejection, depression, need for self-gratification, etc. Let's look at I Corinthians 13:4–8, which explains God's kind of love. Love never fails. Faith, hope, and love abides and the greatest is love (I Corinthians 13:13). I Corinthians 14:1 tells us to follow after love and desire spiritual gifts.

Love and forgiveness go hand in hand. We must at times forgive by faith, just as we accepted our salvation. Whenever a reminder of the wrong comes to our minds we must cast it down and choose to think on other things. Look at Ephesians 4:29–32. If we hold grudges or unforgiveness toward others, then we will have trouble forgiving ourselves. As long as we walk in unforgiveness, we don't have peace. If we don't have peace then we are in torment and every little thing will cause us to react. I Peter 3:7 shows how our prayers can be hindered if we don't walk in love with our spouse. Remember, faith works by love (Galatians 5:6), and so if our prayers aren't being answered, we should look at who we are holding a grudge against.

6 Forgiveness

The hardest thing for our natural mind is to understand or accept God's forgiveness. We look at the sin and automatically think it is an unpardonable sin. This is not true; Jesus died on the cross for all sin (past, present, and future). If He didn't die for future sins, we could never have been saved. God doesn't grade on a curve. Our salvation is not based on what we have done (performance), but rather whether we have accepted His gift of eternal life (John 3:16 and Ephesians 2:8, 9). Do not voice your answer to this question out loud. "What sin is keeping you from fellowship with the Father (war crime, murder, abuse, adultery, etc.)?" Review Chapter V where we discussed God's forgiveness being poured out on David, Peter, and Saul (Paul). God has not changed (Malachi 3:6, Hebrews 13:8, and James 1:17). Once we confess our sin, He remembers it no more (Zephaniah 3:17 and Psalms 103:12) and He cleanses us from all unrighteousness (I John 1:9). It is important to forgive in order that our prayers are answered (Matthew 5:23, 24, 18:21–35, Mark 11:25 and Colossians 3:12, 13).

7 Spirit Soul, and Body

We are a three-part being (spirit, soul, and body), created in God's image. When we received Jesus as our Lord and Savior our spirit was instantly changed. Our soul is comprised of mind, will, and emotions, and it is clear that our body houses the spirit and soul. It is important to understand that upon salvation we become a new creation and receive the spirit of Christ.

When you received Jesus as your Lord and Savior you received His spirit. At this very moment you have the spirit of Christ and can walk as He did. Our mind says, "How is this possible?" It is possible by renewing our mind by meditating on the Word (Romans 12:1, 2). When the mind has been renewed by the Word, it comes into agreement with your spirit, and they will dominate your body. The opposite is true if we let our senses (sight, hearing, taste, smell, touch) dominate rather than the Word (II Corinthians 5:7). Look at Galatians 5:22 and see what is already available in our transformed spirit.

We must continually renew our mind with the Word. As your mind goes, so will your body. Meditate on the Word and have a good life or meditate on things of the world and have a rocky road.

When we sin, it is our flesh that sins, not our spirit. Once we have received Jesus as our Savior, we have the same spirit as Christ. Sin comes from a thought, which is meditated on until it is conceived and acted on. The only way to not carry through with the negative thought is to cast down the vain imagination (II Corinthians 10:3–5) and choose to think on things that are lovely, just, pure, and of a good report (Philippians 4:8). The battle is in our soul (mind) and we have the ability to take control of these thoughts. What do you want for your life (depression, isolation, anxiety, no relationships, etc.)? It is our choice because we have the ability to control our thoughts. Do we stop the negative thoughts before they have a foothold, or do we meditate on them and have a bad day? There is no "justification." We control the mind and the outcome.

8 Knowing Him

James 4:8 tells us to draw nigh to Him and He will draw nigh to us. He has made the provision, through Jesus, and it is up to us to complete the cycle. It says in Revelation 4:11 that we were created for His pleasure. Just as God walked and had fellowship with Adam and Eve in the garden, He desires that same relationship with us. Jesus has come and provides the avenue to have that relationship with God the Father. Look at John 15, which talks about abiding in the vine (Jesus being the vine). Ephesians 1:3 tells us that we have received all spiritual blessings, but we need to see them manifest into the physical realm. This will only come as we spend time meditating the scriptures and in prayer (Romans 12:1 and 2). We must study the Word to show ourselves approved. Look back at Matthew 4:4 when Jesus was tempted. Each time He replied with, "It is written…" and the devil left Him. We can't just hear the Word once and expect it to manifest in our life. We must meditate on the Word and keep in daily fellowship with the Lord. Look at Romans 12:1, 2 and 10:9, 10. Meditating the Word drives out unbelief and brings about faith. Remember, the scripture says Faith comes by hearing and by hearing the Word of God. Whatever you are struggling with, healing, depression, anxiety, fear, etc., the answer is in the Word of God. We have to take the effort. Our spiritual growth is no different than our regular knowledge base growth; it is through study and repetition of whatever we want to learn. Think back on your schooling and how at the beginning of each year there was an overview of what was learned the previous year and we have maintained that knowledge by using it over and over in our daily life. It is no different with the Word of God. To see change in our lives, we must renew our mind and then take the steps required to see the change. We can work toward the change or stay where we are.

9 Authority of the Believer

This week we will start looking at the authority of the believer. What is authority? Authority is delegated power. The authority I'm talking about is that which we have been given as a believer to overcome all situations. Knowing our authority again comes from fellowship with the Lord on a daily basis in prayer and the Word. Let's look at some scriptures to pray over ourselves on a daily basis. As we pray these scriptures, insert "me" where "you" is found. Praying these scriptures over yourself will benefit you and bring revelation of the Word (Ephesians 1:16–20, 3:14–19).

Ephesians 6:12 tells us who the fight is against. Jesus told us that we shall know the truth, and the truth shall set us free (John 8:32). Let's look at Hosea 4:6 and see what the prophet told the children of Israel. Knowledge brings understanding and that is why the scriptures in Ephesians 1:16–20 and Ephesians 3:14–19 are so important to pray.

Luke 10:19 tells us of our authority and in Matthew 28:18, 19 we are told what to do with this authority. As a believer, we must realize that what Jesus did for us goes further than the cross. He is no longer on the cross, but seated at the right hand of the Father. Let's look at the following scriptures before continuing with the study of Ephesians: I John 4:4, I Peter 5:8–9, Colossians 2:15, I Corinthians 12:12–14 and 27, Romans 5:17 and John 14:12.

Now let's go back to chapter 1 of Ephesians and start a verse by verse study. This book tells us not only what Jesus has done for us, but also our authority.

10 Power of the Tongue

Let's look at what Jesus said about our words and how they are related to the heart (Luke 6:45). This week we are going to look at how our tongue controls our life (James 3:1–10). Look at Proverbs 18:20, 21 and how death and life are in the tongue. The book of Proverbs is often called the book of wisdom and talks a lot about the tongue.

The children of Israel wandered in the wilderness for forty years because of their unbelief, which led to murmuring and complaining (I Corinthians 10:5–10. God had delivered them from Egypt, but Egypt was still in their hearts. Do we want to be like the children of Israel and not walk in the blessings? Go to Mark 11:23, 24 and we can see that Jesus stressed "saying" three times. Our words have a very important part in our life's outcome. We are believing God but sowing mixed seed. Remember what James said about a spring having both sweet and bitter water. Every time we speak contrary to what the Word of God has promised, it is like the farmer sowing thistles among his crop. In a field the weeds will overtake the crop unless cultivated. This is exactly what we must do as believers. We must guard our hearts. If we are constantly watching or listening to negative things, then guess what will come out of our mouth when we speak. As believers we want to respond to every situation as Jesus would, and this again comes only by fellowship with the Lord either in prayer or the Word. Remember, it goes back to Romans 12:1–2, renewing our minds.

Scriptures:

Proverbs 4:4, 6:2, 10:19, 10:31–32, 11:9, 11:11, 12:6, 12:14, 12:22, 13:2–3, 14:18, 14:23, 15:1–2, 15:4, 15:7,
15:14, 15:23, 15:26, 15:28, 16:23–24, 16:28, 17:9, 17:27–28, 18:4, 18:6–8, 20:19, 21:23, 23:15–16, 24:1, 26:18, 26:20, and 26:22.
II Timothy 2:16
I Peter 3:10

11 Importance of the Word

Let's continue looking at the importance of our words. This is a review but very important in our Christian lives.

The scriptures are given by God as a handbook and can be used to determine our destiny. The world was created by the Word of God (Genesis 1) and even the conception of Jesus (Luke 1:27–38). This week we will review scriptures that will establish the importance of the Word and enlighten us to the power of God's Word. This is the basic background and without it we can't comprehend God's love or his salvation (freedom from sin, deliverance, healing, and prosperity).

Scripture References:

Genesis 1 (take note of "God said")

Luke 1:27–38 (Gabriel was God's mouthpiece)

John 1:1, John 1:14, I John 5:7, I Peter 1:23–25, Mark 13:31, Matthew 4:4, Psalms 119:89, and Romans 10:17.

We have looked at these scriptures and can see the importance of God's Word. Now let's look at Mark 4:1–20 and see what influence God's Word has on our personal life. Remember Romans 10:17 says, "Faith comes by hearing and hearing by the Word of God." Last scripture reference is John 8:31, 32, which relates to Mark 4:1–20 we just read.

12 Confession

Let's look at Mark 11:23, 24 again. It is easy to read the scriptures, but sometimes we ask, "Will it work for me?" First we must remember that Jesus is not a respecter of persons. He loves you and wants nothing but good for your life. We have choices to make and sometimes they are the wrong choices. The good thing is that Jesus is full of mercy and grace. He knew what choices we would make and has already made provision for our forgiveness, deliverance, healing, and prosperity. Generally the problem lies one inch below our nose. We say we believe but at the same time speak to the contrary. Look at James chapter 3 verses 1–12. When you want the cat do you call the dog? We must line the words of our mouth up with what we are believing. We can easily blame the devil for hindering our prayer or manifestation but usually it is our own confession. For example, when around fellow believers we quote scriptures and faith filled words, but when around unbelievers or even alone, we speak words of doubt and unbelief. "By His stripes I'm healed." "My head is throbbing; I need something for the pain!" Which is it? Are you healed or are you in pain? Remember what James had to say. Look at the following scriptures: I Peter 3:10, Hebrews 4:14, and I Timothy 6:12. There are many scriptures throughout Proverbs that refer to the tongue, which you can read on your own.

Below is a sample confession that I do over my body. It can be modified for each individual and what they are believing God for. It is good to confess this until it becomes revelation and you must believe that God is a rewarder of those who diligently seek Him.

Father, I thank you for being my Creator and my Lord. I give You all praise and glory. I thank You for your healing power and that what You have created You can repair. According to Your Word in Mark 11:23, 24 "Whatsoever I desire and ask in Your name, believing in my heart, and confessing with my mouth, You will do it," I ask and thank You for doing the following. I speak to my brain and command it to produce the right amount of chemicals for the time and situation. I thank you that I am not dependent on medication to keep the chemicals in balance but that You keep the chemicals in balance. I speak to my lungs and command them to inhale the proper amount of oxygen and exhale the proper amount of carbon dioxide. Lungs you are free of any foreign matter and strong and healthy. I speak to my circulatory system and command it to function as designed. I command my heart muscle to be strong with no blemish. I speak to every valve, artery, vein, and capillary to be normal. I command blood pressure to be normal, without medication, at 120/70. I command any plaque build up to dissolve immediately and cholesterol to be normal. I speak to my urinary tract and command it to be normal. Bladder, you will hold the correct amount and not grow weak as I age but function as designed. Kidneys, you will filter as designed with no formation of kidney stones. You will continually have normal lab reports with the correct parameters on all levels. I speak to my liver and command normal enzyme levels, normal viral count, and no enlargement at all. I speak to my reproductive system and command wholeness. Prostate I command any enlargement to leave now. I speak to my PSA and command all readings to be normal. I come against any growths or foreign substance on my prostate and thank you for normal sexual functioning. I speak to my gall bladder and command it to be normal and stone free. I thank You that I can eat whatever I desire with no acid reflux, heart burn, etc.

I thank You, Father, for Your provision of healing and divine health even though in the natural some of these conditions were my fault. I thank You for being a loving God, full of mercy and grace. I curse any and all outside influences on my body. I command all negative symptoms to leave my body now in the name of Jesus. It is not by my works, but rather by the stripes of Jesus that my body is healed from the top of my head to the bottom of my feet. I thank You for the long life that You have promised me and the opportunity to serve You. I ask and thank You in the name of Jesus (John 15:7). Amen.

13 Dealing with Anger

This week we are going to start looking at scriptural ways of dealing with those PTSD symptoms. Anger is an emotion that more times than not will get you into trouble. Anger is usually displayed toward anyone around you at the time you have an incident. Let's look at the first display of anger recorded in the Bible (Genesis 3:8–13) Adam was angry with what he was about to lose and started blaming, "it was that woman." Adam wouldn't take responsibility for his own action or the deceit of the woman. Next, Genesis 4:5–8. We see here that Cain was both jealous and angry which led him to kill Abel. Anger is an emotion that can be controlled. It is started in the mind and then acted on. Who is in control of your mind? The Word tells us to "Submit yourself to God, resist the devil and he will flee (James 4:7)." Adam was given dominion over the earth and

Jesus gave back the authority when He died and went to Hell. He stripped the devil of everything and gave all power and authority back to us (Colossians 2:15). I have said it over and over (Romans 12:1, 2), we must renew our mind with the Word of God. Another place where anger took control was in Genesis 27:41–45. Esau's anger turned to hate and he plotted to kill Jacob (Genesis 49:5–7).

Here are some scriptures dealing with anger. Look at the warnings and what anger/wrath can cost you. It is our choice. We can keep the anger and lose our friends or family. We will see that anger is often associated with a foolish man.

Proverbs 10:19, 15:1, 2, 15:18, 16:32, 17:27, 28, 18:2, 18:6, 7,19:11, 19:19, 22:8, 22:24, 27:3, 4, 29:8, 11, 29:20, 29:22, 30:33

Ecclesiastes 7:9, Colossians 3:8–10, 3:21, Ephesians 4:26, 4:31, 6:4, I Timothy 2:8, Titus 1:7, and James 1:19, 20.

If we really look at all the PTSD symptoms, they are based off the main one of anger. We isolate/withdraw because we can't deal with people. We can tie in family relationships also. Anger has been used to control and give the warning to stay away. Depression comes from anger not dealt with and turned inwards. Survivors guilt carries on because we are either angry because a friend was killed or question why it wasn't me. You can look at the other symptoms and see how the anger affects them. It is time to really search our soul and address these issues once and for all. The true answer comes from the Word of God. Look at Philippians 3:13, 14. It is possible to forget those things that happened but it is our choice. How bad do you want it is the question. The more you read and meditate the scriptures the more your deliverance.

14 Conquering Emotions and Stress

This week we will look at how to master our emotions and how to conquer stress. Why are we content only to manage our stress/ emotions? Wouldn't you rather master or dominate stress which causes our emotions to rule. Your emotions determine the outcome of your life based on the decisions you make. A chemical imbalance is caused by stressors in your life, which in turn can cause depression, anxiety, etc. The person with a chemical imbalance, if seen by a doctor, is placed on medication to correct the chemical imbalance, although the medication generally has numerous side effects. Your emotions are subject to your control. We can choose to let our emotions control us and others or we can choose to control the emotions. Oftentimes how we feel generates how we react to a situation. Remember that we are a three part being: spirit, soul, and body. Our emotions are found in the soul or mind and influence our body.

We have looked at this passage of scriptures in a previous Bible study, but it proves the point very well of being ruled by emotions. Let's look at the first recorded incident where a person's emotion of anger caused a murder (Genesis 4:1–10). As we read these scriptures, God was pleased with Abel's sacrifice and not Cain's sacrifice. This generated anger to rise up in Cain, who then murdered Abel. The scriptures point out how Cain was angered, his countenance changed, and he gave way to sin. Romans 6:14 tells us "For sin shall not have dominion over you, for you are not under law but under grace." Cain talked to Abel before getting his emotions under control, which led to murder. Cain was ruled by his emotions as many are today. His emotion of anger caused a physical change which when not dealt with caused an outward action. We must always remember that consequences follow our actions (good or bad). We should never confront someone without having our emotions under control, lest we lose a friend or create a bad relationship. The veteran diagnosed with PTSD often thinks that he has no control over his emotions, anger outbursts, depression, anxiety, etc. and oftentimes uses them to control others, not a Godly trait. Depression comes from anger turned inward. Hope deferred makes a heart sick (Proverbs 13:4).

Isaiah 26:3 says that "*Lord* you will keep him in perfect peace, whose mind is stayed on thee." When we choose to think on things that are true, noble, just, pure, lovely, and of a good report (Philippians 4:8), we will keep our emotions under control. Being

117

ruled by our emotions is the opposite of being faith ruled. We walk by faith and not by sight (II Corinthians 5:7). We need to base our decisions on what outcome we desire rather than our emotions. Meditation on a thought produces the emotion, which brings a reaction to the emotion. We have the ability to cast down those negative thoughts, (I Corinthians 10:3–5). This can be easily demonstrated by counting to ten silently, and as you count, say your name. What happened to your counting? The spoken word stopped the thought process of counting. This is true in every area; the spoken Word of God will counter your thought pattern. John 6:63 shows us to be spiritually minded is to be Word minded, which comes only from meditating on God's Word. Jesus said, "Let not your heart be troubled" (John 14:1). If He tells us not to let our hearts be troubled, then it must be possible. We must continually think on God's Word and put it first place in our life. Out of the abundance of the heart the mouth speaks. Are you speaking God's Word or the problem? Go back and review Mark chapter 4 and the sower sows the Word. You must take a stand and be prepared to fight the fight of faith. Remember John 10:10. Are you seeing the abundant life?

Are we exempt from ever having a trial or tribulation? Let's look at John 16:33, Psalms 34:19 and II Corinthians 4:8–9. These scriptures point out that we will have trouble, but will be delivered. How are we delivered? Look at James 3:2. The tongue controls our whole body. So speak to the mountain. You have the authority. Don't be passive.

Many things cause stress in your life: uncertainty, unresolved conflict, unrealistic comparison, unconfessed sin, unusual pressure, indecisiveness, etc.

How to deal with stress: (Philippians 4:6–8). We must always pray with thanksgiving in all situations. As mentioned many times before, renewing our mind is important (Romans 12:1, 2). To get Word results, we must do what the Word says. You can be in control of your emotions or you can let your emotions control you. It is your decision.

15 Healing

Healing is a provision of the atonement. Jesus bore stripes on His back to provide for our healing. Healing was provided for in the Old Testament as well. Look at Exodus 15:26. If you look at the deliverance from bondage in Egypt, there was not one sick among the Israelites. The first Passover was when the Israelites prepared to leave and were told to kill the lamb, eat it, and place blood on the doorpost. This was a signal for the death angel to pass over the house. Throughout the Old Testament God continually told of His healing power and ability. God has always wanted His children well.

References:

Isaiah 53:3–5, Psalms 103:1–5, 107–20, Proverbs 4:21, 22, and Jeremiah 30:17.

When Jesus came it was no different. Look at Luke 4:17–19. He came to heal, deliver, and set the captive free. This can be seen throughout His ministry on the earth.

References:

Matthew 4:23, 24, 6:10, 8:1–3, 5–10, 13, 14–17, 28–33, 9:1–8, 18–25, 27–31, 32–35, 10:1, 5–8, 11:1–5, 12:9–15, 22, 14:13, 14, 34–36, 15:21–28, 29–31, 17:14–18, 19:1, 2, 20:29–34, and 21:14.

I have given you the healing scriptures from the book of Matthew. The best way to learn the Bible is to read it and look things up for yourself. Over the next couple of weeks, look up the healing scriptures in the next three Gospels and write down the references and we will look at them together the next time. As you look at them some of the recordings will show the other writers' perspective on the healing. The different perspective doesn't change the fact that Jesus healed everyone who came to Him in faith, not doubting. Hebrews 13:8 says, "Jesus is the same yesterday, today, and forever." He healed then and still heals today.

Mark 1:21–27, 29–31, 32–34, 39–44, 2:1–12, 3:1–5, 9–11, 14, 15, 5:1–16, 21–43, 6:1–7, 12–13, 53–56, 7:24–30, 31–37, 8:22–25, 9:14–29, 10:46–52, and 16:15–18.

Luke 4:18, 19, 32–36, 38–41, 5:12–15, 17–26, 6:5–10, 17–19, 7:1–16, 21, 22, 8:1, 2, 26–36, 40–56, 9:1, 2, 6, 11, 37–43, 49, 50, 10:8, 9, 19, 11:14, 13:10–13, 16, 18:35–43, 22:48–51.
John 4:46–54, 5:1–15, 21, 6:2, 9:1–33, 11:31–45, 12:1
Acts 3:1–12, 16, 4:5–10, 14, 21, 22, 5:15

Remember John 10:10, "The thief comes to steal, kill, and destroy but I have come to give life and life more abundantly." If it isn't creating abundant life, then it isn't from God. If you believe that God gave you or caused an illness then you can't have faith to be healed. You are going against the will of God if you believe He gave you the sickness, and you go to the doctor to get better. Sickness came as a result of the fall of man.

16 Count It All Joy!

What is our reaction to a tragedy, whether national or personal? Do we meditate on the tragedy until we go into a depression or do we look at what the scriptures have to say? Here again it is our decision as to how we react. Meditate on the problem and be depressed or meditate on the Word and see victory. Let's look at some scriptures regarding joy (James 1:2, and Job 5:22).

In Philippians Paul mentions joy and rejoicing 16 times. He wrote this while in prison. He didn't choose to look at the circumstances but rather at God's provision. He encouraged others on how to get through the rough times. He really had a revelation of Philippians 3:13, 14 and we must get the same revelation.

Philippians 1:3, 4, 15–18, 25, 26, 2:2,14–18, 27–29, 3:1, 3,4:1, 4, 10
Nehemiah 8:10 (joy of the Lord is my strength)
Habakkuk 3:17–19
I Peter 1:8 (yet believing, rejoice)
Romans 14:17 The kingdom of God is righteousness, peace, and joy in the Holy Ghost.
Genesis 21:6 (the Lord made me laugh)
Hebrews 11:11 (conceived by faith)

Genesis 26:12 (sowed in the time of famine) This scripture shows that even though all natural things were against Isaac that God was above the circumstances. We must remember that God is no respecter of persons. What he has done for one, He will do for you. It is up to you as to what you sow and reap. The farmer sows corn to reap corn, wheat for wheat, beans for beans, etc. When we sow mercy and grace, we receive mercy and grace in return. The sowing and reaping is also in our mind. If we constantly think on negative and depressing things, we will see negative things happen and be depressed. The decision is ours, and no matter how much medication we take, it will not change that. Medication is a mask but the thoughts are real. Think of a child's Halloween mask. The child was the same, but appeared as someone else. Taking medication and not changing our thoughts, which cause the depression, does not get to the root.

We must hold on to the promises of God, no matter what the situation. Whatever we are going through is temporal and subject to change (II Corinthians 4:18).

We can look at David and see how he chose to rejoice no matter the circumstance. In II Samuel 6:12–23 we see how David stripped himself of his royal garments and danced before the Lord. He was an example to the people and showed true humility. Even though David did many things wrong he knew where his strength came from and was quick to repent and praise God.

Psalms 2:4, 5, 11, 12 (fullness of joy)

Do we want to live a depressed life or one of fullness and joy? It all comes back to our decisions. The veteran is no different than any other person suffering with depression. The decision is ours—to live with it or continue on with our lives. It has been thirty years since Vietnam. Isn't it time to lay it to rest? Forgiveness is the greatest release that a person will ever know. It frees you to love and enjoy life. We can't go back and change the past but we can move on and live a joyous life. Life is too short not to enjoy every minute of it with family and friends.

17 Giving

This week we are going to look at giving and it may not agree with what you have been taught. Listen with an open heart and ask any questions. As we study the Bible we can see God's principles of giving. The first scriptures on giving are in Genesis 3:21 and right after the fall of man. Throughout the Old Testament we can find numerous scriptures related to giving and most of them related to a sin offering. We can see that giving is related to as seed time and harvest (Genesis 8:22). Once the tribe of Levi was established as the priesthood with the job of taking care of the temple, their support came by means of the tithe and offerings. They were instructed as to what was given to the Lord and what was their portion. Their portion was to feed them as well as the widows, orphans, and those travelling through the land. The more you sow, the larger crop you harvest (II Corinthians 9:6). This principle isn't just for finances but everything in your life. In Malachi 3:10 it talks about robbing God with the tithe and offerings (tithe meaning tenth). People don't really like to hear this today because they don't think they can make it if they give. On the contrary, once we learn why we give, we are blessed back. Let's look at Deuteronomy 8:11–18 which tells us why he gives us the ability to gain wealth. Now let's go to Acts 4:34–37 and see what the New Testament church did. Paul in II Corinthians 9:6 instructs us on how to give. Now let's look at these final scriptures, I Corinthians 13:1–3, and evaluate what our motive for giving should be. Two other scriptures that prove this out are John 3:16 and John 15:13. We can see in both of these scriptures that love was first and giving accompanied this love. We love Jesus, and thus, we want to give in order to see others come into the kingdom. This is also revealed in Luke 19:1–10, where Zacchaeus desired to see Jesus so much that he climbed a tree. Jesus stopped, called him down, and said He was going to his house. Zacchaeus upon receiving Jesus announced that he was giving 50% of his wealth to the ministry and repaying anyone he had wronged by four times. Receiving Jesus changes your heart immediately and the desire to give becomes natural. You can't out give God.

Summary:

In Lesson 13 we looked at the scriptures dealing with anger/ wrath, and its warnings. We saw where many times the angry man was related to being a fool. Yes, a fool, because of the actions taken while in a state of anger. We talked about how we are the ones in control of our actions and nobody else. It is easy to point the finger and blame someone else for your actions but that isn't true. Remember Adam in the Garden, he blamed God and Eve. Eve blamed the serpent. Both pointed the finger rather than taking responsibility. Why is it so hard to take responsibility? We blame our wife, children, friends, government, the war, etc.

As veterans, who served during a war, we all had different experiences. It is our decision as to how those experiences are going to affect our lives. We can either use our war experience as an excuse for our actions or we can look at the real issue, ourselves. While in the service, fight or flight was instilled in our lives. In combat it was good and kept us alive, but today we aren't in those life or death situations. We must evaluate each situation that arises and react accordingly. How can we do this? By filling yourself with the Word of God. When the Word of God becomes first place in your life, you will see change. Let's go back and look at Mark 4:1–20 and the sower sows the Word. Evaluate your life and see where you fit in this parable. If you aren't where you would like to be, then change it. This change will only come by fellowship with the Father through prayer and the Word.

Remember the stronghold is in the mind and we have control over our mind. If you don't like what you are seeing in your life, then change it. You say "I have tried but it doesn't work." You haven't tried changing your thoughts by meditating on the Word of God, because it doesn't fail. If we took as much time meditating on God's Word as we do the problem, we wouldn't have the problem. Questions for each of us to answer ourselves: Do we use the diagnosis of PTSD as an excuse to act out? Do we want to continue our lives in depression, anger, withdrawn, etc? Think on these questions and answer them only to yourself. The healing will come when we are ready to move on and put the war experience behind us. God is love and wants us to be in health and prosper (3 John 2). It comes back to responsibility. What type of ground are you, and are you willing to change?

Mary and I pray that the information contained in this book has helped the reader to understand the torment that plagues our soldiers after the war and the way to freedom from it. The Biblical teachings and references throughout the book have healed me, delivered me, and are continually restoring my soul. Remember that God is no respecter of persons and what God has done for me, He will do for you. God bless you and thank you for your service to God and our country.

Printed in the United States
50589LVS00002B/25-126